THE TWELVE

The "Minor" Prophets Speak Today

Biblical Character Studies by Walter C. Kaiser, Jr.

The Lives and Ministries of ELIJAH and ELISHA

ABRAHAM The Friend of God

JOSHUA A True Servant Leader

JOSEPH From Prison to Palace

The Journey from JACOB to Israel

NEHEMIAH The Wall Builder

SAMUEL The Seer
First In the Prophetic Movement in Israel

THE TWELVE The "Minor" Prophets Speak Today

— ✡ —

Coming Soon

DAVID A Man After God's Own Heart

MOSES The Man Who Saw the Invisible God

SOLOMON The King with a Listening Heart

ZECHARIAH The Quintessence of Old Testament Prophecy

DANIEL The Handwriting is on the Wall

RUTH The Moabite and the Providence of God
and
ESTHER God Preserves the Jewish Nation

THE TWELVE

The "Minor" Prophets Speak Today

Walter C. Kaiser, Jr.

Lederer Books
an imprint of
Messianic Jewish Publishers
Clarksville, MD 21029

Unless otherwise noted, all Scripture quotations are taken from the New American Standard Bible. Nashville: Thomas Nelson Publishers, 1978; the Complete Jewish Bible, Baltimore: Messianic Jewish Publishers, 1998; or the New International Version Bible, New York: International Bible Society, 2002.

Special thanks to Brian A. Kaiser
for creating the maps showing the travels of Elijah and Elisha.
Cover design by Lisa Rubin,
Messianic Jewish Publishers
Graphic Design by Yvonne Vermillion,
MagicGraphix.com

ISBN 978-1-951833-10-7

Library of Congress Control Number: 2019944024

Published by:
Lederer Books
An imprint of Messianic Jewish Publishers
6120 Day Long Lane
Clarksville, MD 21029

Distributed by:
Messianic Jewish Publishers & Resources
Order line: (800) 410-7367
lederer@messianicjewish.net
www.MessianicJewish.net

DEDICATION

For the Wonderful Students of
THE BILLY GRAHAM TRAINING CENTER AT THE COVE
IN
Asheville, North Carolina
June 26-30, 2017

Table of Contents

Introduction

Should Believers Major On The Minor Prophets?

In addition to the twelve minor prophets, placed at the end of English versions of the Older Testament, there were many more non-writing prophets. Apparently only a few of the prophets have been chosen to be included as biblical text by the Spirit of God.

Our knowledge of the prophets comes from two sources: those who left no writings, but whose names and or activities are known from the historical books (such as Joshua, Judges, Samuel and Kings); the others are known to us from the books written and named after them. Even those who had books named after them may not have been the authors of those books, for the prophets were primarily preachers and activists rather than authors, so there is a strong chance they may have used amanuenses.

The group of writing prophets have usually been organized into what we now call the "major prophets" and "minor prophets," a distinction not referring to the importance or significance of the prophet. It referred only to the general size and length of the books. Thus, the major prophets were longer books (i.e., Isaiah 66 chapters, Jeremiah 52 chapters, Ezekiel 48 chapters, Daniel 12 chapters), while all twelve of the minor prophets made up a total of only 67 chapters.

The twelve Minor Prophets, in the order they are generally presented are: Hosea, Joel, Amos, Obadiah, Jonah, Micah, Nahum, Habakkuk, Zephaniah, Haggai, Zechariah, and Malachi. The designation for these shorter books from early Christian and Jewish sources was "The Book of the Twelve" or "the Twelve Prophets" or just "The Minor Prophets" (*Ecclesiasticus* 49:10; *Josephus, Apion* I.8; *Eusebius* H.E. 4.26.14; *Augusti ne, City of God* 18.29).

Ancient Jewish "books" were often written on scrolls, composed of either long rolled strips of pressed papyrus or parchment. A major prophet would fit his entire book on one long scroll extending up to some 35 feet long, but all twelve minor prophets fit on a single such scroll.

Understanding the Prophets

A prophet, of course, was a man called by God and moved by God's Spirit (Deut. 18:15-22; 2 Pet. 1:20-21). There were a few women "prophetesses" as well, but none of them wrote books included in scripture (e.g., Miriam, Hannah, and Anna). The prophet was not to use his position to introduce new and strange religions or theology (Deut. 13:1-5), nor was his calling to introduce a new law; instead, their function was to call men and women back to the word God had given to Moses and to pray for the people he served. The new words taught by the prophet were to agree with what had already been revealed by God.

A prophet was not to speak on his own authority; rather he was to speak only in the name of and on the authority of the LORD. That prophet should be able to accompany the words he taught with signs and wonders that would authenticate that word as being from God. Moreover, the truthfulness of a prophet's ability to predict the future was to be seen in the fulfillment of near-term events that he predicted. If these came to pass, then his long-range projections into the future could be trusted. The short-term fulfillments were the reasons their audiences were able to trust their long-range predictions (Deut. 18:15-22). In this way, the more immediate fulfillments confirmed the truthfulness of those in the future.

Often the prophecies carried conditions with them, based on how the people responded to the prophet's words (Jer. 18:5-11). Yet, some oracles were unconditional, relying entirely on God for their fulfillment. Examples of such unconditional predictions were God's promise to the seasons (Gen. 8:22), or his promise about the New Heavens and New Earth (Isa. 65:17-23), or his declaration of justification by faith alone (Gen. 15:6).

Another divine promise, made to the Patriarchs, was about electing Israel as his people, giving them the Land of Israel, and making them a channel of blessing to all the world. The prophet's audience knew that most other oracles had a suppressed, "unless you repent," aspect to them (See Jonah).

Significant Dates and Arrangements of the Books

It will be helpful to keep these key dates in mind as you study these twelve books:

722/721 B.C.E. The Fall of Samaria and collapse of the Ten Northern Tribes of Israel as they were led into exile in Assyria.

611 B.C.E. The Fall of Nineveh to the Babylonians.

606 B.C.E. The Battle of Carchemish where the Babylonians became dominant in Ancient Near East from that time forward.

597 B.C.E. Nebuchadnezzar's first victory over Jerusalem and the exile of King Johoiachin.

586 B.C.E. Nebuchadnezzar's third and final destruction of Jerusalem and his exile of most of the remaining Judeans to Babylon.

539 B.C.E. The beginning of the Persian hegemony in Near East.

536 B.C.E. Cyrus's decree permits Jewish return from exile and the reconstruction of the destroyed Temple. Return led by Governor Zerubbabel and High Priest Joshua.

520 B.C.E. God sends two prophets, Haggai and Zechariah, to stir up people to resume work on the Temple.

516 B.C.E. Work completed on the Temple and the Second Temple is dedicated.

457 B.C.E. A second return to Israel led by Ezra.

445 B.C.E. Nehemiah leads a third return to Jerusalem and rebuilds the walls around her.

Arrangement of the books according to their general historical periods. Note the century each prophet preached in.

Ninth Century	Eighth Century	Seventh Century	Sixth-Fifth Century
Joel	Jonah	Zephaniah	Haggai
Amos	Habakkuk	Zechariah	Obadiah
Hosea	Nahum	Malachi	Micah

The Literary Types of the Twelve

Among the twelve books, there is a wide range of literary types. For example, Hosea and Amos exhibit a combination of stories about the prophet, along with collections of their oracles. Conversely, the book of Jonah is almost totally about his personal story. A very small part of the content was about what he preached. Yet, Nahum is composed entirely of the prophet's preaching, addressed to the same people to whom Jonah preached. Zechariah uses almost one half of his book for visions, but then concludes with strong preaching on what God will do in the future "Day of the Lord." Malachi engages in a series of arguments between him and his audience, using disputations for a format. Habakkuk raises the deep discussion of theodicy with God, but still shows how to wait patiently on him and his word. Haggai is most careful to date each of his messages, which is rather unique, since none of the other twelve do.

Earliest Manuscript Evidence for the Twelve

In 1947, a mega change came in the study of the "Older" Testament. A chance discovery by a Bedouin goatherd, in the area of the Dead Sea caves, on the west side of the Dead Sea, produced some of the earliest Hebrew manuscripts, 1,000 years older than the texts previously possessed. They have been named the Dead Sea Scrolls (DSS). That discovery touched off a search of other caves, eleven more yielding a total of some 900 Hebrew Biblical texts.

In Cave 1 there was almost the full text of Habakkuk, along with a commentary, and fragments of Hosea and Nahum. Cave 2 had scraps of Jonah and cave 4 parts of all the minor prophets except Obadiah, Habakkuk and Haggai. The other caves yielded fragments from all the Twelve.

These discoveries move us much closer to the full collecrtion of these manuscripts. They have been a real godsend to the study of the text of these prophets. It is my hope that the study of these twelve lessons will stimulate numerous Bible studies in many lands today. God bless you and reward you for your investment in God's word, for he will never disappoint you.

Lesson 1

HOSEA

The Prophet of the Love of God

The First of the Twelve

Hosea is the author of the book that is placed at the head of the Scriptures labeled by Augustine as "The Minor Prophets," but they were also known in the Jewish world as *Shneim Asar,* the "Twelve Prophets," or just "The Twelve." Hosea's ministry was addressed to the northern ten tribes, as was the ministry of the prophet Amos, but unlike Amos, who came from the south, Hosea also lived in the northern part of Israel.

The Man Hosea

Hosea, whose name means "salvation," was a prophet who experienced the deep agonies of a broken marriage after his wife left him. His ministry took place shortly before the fall of Samaria in 721 B.C.E. (Hos. 1:4), which was the capital of the northern ten tribes. Therefore, Hosea was a contemporary with the prophets Isaiah, Jonah, Micah, and Amos. Yet in his own experiences, he learned firsthand how God himself must have been deeply hurt by his people when they abandoned their God, much as Hosea's wife Gomer abandoned him and their marriage as she had left Hosea to give her love and affection to the idols of false religion and to men of loose morals.

The Times of This Book

In the superscription to his book (1:1), Hosea names the following kings as reigning during his ministry as a prophet: Uzziah, Jotham, Ahaz and Hezekiah, who were kings in Judah; and King Jeroboam II (ca. 786–746 B.C.E.), who ruled in northern Israel. Since Hosea makes no reference to the Syro-Ephraimite War (735–733), nor does he note the fall of Samaria in his writing as an event that has already happened (721), his work must have happened just before this war, slightly preceding the key events of 721.

It is strange that even though Hosea worked in the northern kingdom of Israel, he named four of the kings of Judah in the south, but only one king in the north, covering that same period, making no reference to the six last kings of the northern kingdom (2 Kings 15:8–17:6). There is no explanation for his selection of kings or for his omission of the final kings of northern Israel.

The Title of This Man, Hosea

Interestingly, Hosea is never explicitly called a "prophet" per se in his book; we are merely given his name, the name of his father, Beeri, and the names of some of the kings in Judah and northern Israel. There are, however, seven allusions to "Judah" (1:7; 4:15; 5:5; 8:14; 12:2), where Hosea makes some comparison or contrast between Israel and Judah, but his ministry was in the north and not directed primarily to the south.

The Genre of the Book of Hosea

It is important to note that within the "Book of the Twelve," i.e., in the Minor Prophets, only three of these writers use the genre of a narrative format, namely: the book of Jonah, the prophecy of Habakkuk, and the opening three chapters of Hosea. But this narrative is set in a Hebrew grammatical form that must be interpreted very closely, lest a false view of marriage leniency is attributed to God and to the prophet Hosea.

The unusual introduction to the book of Hosea is stated this way: "When the LORD began to speak through Hosea" (Hebrew, *tehillat dibber Yahweh b'Hoshea`*, meaning "the beginning of the word of the LORD through Hosea") (1:2). The Hebrew construct noun rendered "at the beginning" (or "at the first") is critical to correctly interpreting this text. By using this form, Hosea causes us to look back with him on his story to the time when he began his ministry and as he was told to marry Gomer, who at that time did become his wife and had not yet entered the worship of foreign gods. (Neither is she to be confused with the modern-day fictional character of Gomer Pyle.)

God's Command to the Prophet Hosea

However, since the prophet is speaking retrospectively of a former day, it seems that in his hurry to get to the content of his message, he linked together God's original command to him with what happened later to that marriage. God's command to him must have gone like this: "Hosea, take to yourself a wife." But this command to marry Gomer collapsed with a statement of what took place later after they had lived together for some time and had a family of three children, with an added statement of how his wife abandoned him and gave herself to harlotry. Thus, Hosea loosely joined the phrase of her adultery with God's earlier command to take a wife, which then became "to marry a wife of harlotry." So he conflated the divine command to "go, take to yourself a wife" with the tragic news of what later took place all into a single command and one sentence, even though the divine command and the later reputation of his wife occurred at some distance apart—his wife became adulterous and unfaithful *after* she had borne Hosea three children and hence the stigma of her harlotry passed, not only on to the prophet's reputation and ministry, difficult as that was, but also that same stigma passed on to their three children, who became known as "children of harlotry" (1:2b), even though we see nothing in the text about any immoral acts committed in the early days of their marriage during which time the children were conceived.

Moreover, the children are described as the precise children of Hosea and Gomer, for the first, Jezreel, was said to have been born as "[Gomer] conceived and bore *to him* [Hosea] a son" (1:3b). The other two children were kids Hosea specifically named, which in those days was the father's unique, exclusive privilege. In this case it was specially said that Hosea named them as symbols of Israel's status with God. So, the three children were Hosea's, yet they got the bad label of being the "children of harlotry"—not because of how they were conceived or when they were born, but because of their mother's later involvement in harlotry.

Thus, as Hosea looked back on his life ("at the first/beginning") much later, he saw the tragedy that had befallen him as part of the story he had to tell. However, Hosea never doubted that the Lord had specifically directed him to marry this very same woman named Gomer, who was not immoral when they married. Nevertheless, in God's divine providence, the

Lord used Hosea's circumstance to teach him, and to educate Israel, about their waywardness and their own persistent sin. This event was so much a part of his life that as he reflected on it, he collapsed the story into one command and one later happening to become one story, making both equal parts of God's command, even though they were separate and happened at separate times and under different circumstances! This command, however, involved both God's command to marry this woman, which came first, and the divine permission to let Gomer sow her wild oats because of her leaving her faith in God. Accordingly, the prophet and his children were both stigmatized, and Gomer's harlotry became part of their family history and a tragic part of their story and the prophet's ministry!

Hosea saw God's purpose and the resulting outcome of his marriage to a wayward Gomer as being so closely and tragically linked together that he quickly apprehended through his own experience as to how grievous the sin of the nation of Israel was to the heart and holiness of God. He learned firsthand what subsequent infidelity and continued unfaithfulness meant to a love and trust that came from our Lord to a wicked nation, and how that which was offered so freely to all of Israel could result in such violent abuse and violation in those who scorned that love and faithfulness—just as Gomer had sabotaged her own marriage. If Hosea's heart had been broken by such a treasonous and unrequited action (and it clearly was), what must the heartbreak of God have been, and continue to be, in even more exceedingly graphic and realistic terms for every other similar case in history.

Hosea and Gomer's First Child – Jezreel

Hosea and Gomer together had three children during the early days of their marriage. The names, moreover, were directly given by God to Hosea to place on the heads of the children. The firstborn was a son, whom God told Hosea to name "Jezreel" (1:4). His name meant "God scatters," as well as "God sows," for the two actions were linked; sowing in those days involved casting or scattering the seed by hand from a bucket carried on the hip of the sower as he walked through the field, scattering the seed out of his hand. The seed fell on the soil even as the sower continued. This involved grabbing the seed from the bucket, then as the sower walked, he would drop the seed with a sweeping motion of his arm to the right and then to the left, as he proceeded through the field. The seed would exit his hand between his thumb and index finger. Thus he "scattered" the seed while simultaneously indeed "sowing" the seed as it fell. This was called "broadcasting" the seed, which relied on the rain to sink into the soil so it could take root.

This name and illustration served God's purposes well, for after he had scattered his people around the world, he would once again sow them back in their own land of Israel in the latter days of this earth. God added in verse 4a that he "would soon punish the house of Jehu for the massacre of [the city of] Jezreel." This may seem a reference to King Jehu's bloody purge of the Baal worship in Jezreel, but for that act he had received a divine commission (2 Kings 10:30). But when Jehu went far beyond what God had authorized him to do, God signaled the end of the Omride dynasty to which Jehu belonged. In fact. the last king in that line, Zechariah, was assassinated by King Shallum (2 Kings 15:8–12), which the Greek translation (the Septuagint) said took place at Ibleam, a town in that same valley of Jezreel.

Hosea and Gomer's Second Child – Lo-Ruhamah

A second child was born to Gomer and Hosea, named "Lo-Ruhamah," meaning "not pitied" (v. 6). This name also had symbolic power, for it seemed to break the relationship that God's Promise-Plan had so frequently affirmed and promised to Israel: "I will be your God and you shall be my people" (e.g., Lev. 26:12). The text does not directly say that Gomer bore this daughter to Hosea, as was clearly said of her brother Jezreel, but as the Lord directly told Hosea to name her "Lo-Ruhamah," she was clearly his child also. Her name, given by God, had a dire meaning for Israel at the time and in the future!

Hosea and Gomer's Third Child – Lo-Ammi

A third child was born to this couple, a boy. The Lord instructed Hosea to name him "Lo-Ammi," meaning "not my people" (v. 9). God had promised way back in Egypt, "I will take you to be my people and I will be your God" (Exod. 6:7). However, because of Israel's unbelief, not all Israel would enjoy the benefits of that relationship. This would not be the end of Israel, for God later turned bad news into marvelous deliverance in the future.

A Marvelous Reminder of God's Ancient Promise

Once the narrative for the naming of the three children had ended, the names of these siblings were sharply increased in significance and shocking contrast with the bright words of hope God said would litter their future (1:10–11). In fact, the words of the naming narrative had ended with the dreadful words of 1:9b, "You are not my people, and I am not your God."

But in place of that sad declaration a divine word came to the prophet with these contrasting words of contrast: "Yet the Israelites will be like the sand on the seashore, which cannot be measured or counted. … They will be called the sons of the living God. The people of Judah and the people of Israel will be reunited, and they will appoint one leader who will come up out of the land, for great will be the day of Jezreel" (1:10–11).

This was but another reminder of the ancient promises God had given to Abraham, Isaac, and Jacob, as well as to David and Solomon. Here were three promises that God would release for this nation:

1. The two kingdoms of the northern ten tribes and the two tribes of Israel in the south would be reunited once more into a single nation that had been divided since the split in 931 B.C.E.

2. The nation Israel would be led by one single leader in that day.

3. The nation Israel would once again control its own land and territory.

But what was the meaning of "Great will be the day of Jezreel?" (1:11). Obviously, the nature of the name "Jezreel" had changed from the days of the excessive and unauthorized murdering of their own people Israel under Omri's dynasty, led by King Jehu, to a day of hope and sowing of the people in the land. And if the name of Jezreel had changed, then so too had the names of the children changed, for now they would "be sown" (as in "Jezreel") and not "scattered" any longer; they would be "pitied" with God's loving kindness and mercy, and they would be called "my people"—not as previously they were known as the "scattered," those "without mercy," and the nation that was "not my people"!

God's words of judgment are then given in 2:2–23. They are directed not just to Gomer, but also to Israel and the nations of the world. However, once more the story of Hosea's life moved forward in time as the three declarations symbolized by the names of the renamed children of what God would do "in that day" (i.e., in eschatological time) appeared in 2:16, 18, 21.

A Second Command from God to Love Gomer Again

Suddenly in Hosea 3:1 Hosea switched from recounting his life's story in the third-person and what had happened in those former days to a new first-person recollection. At some later time, God told him to "Go again, love a woman!" The Hebrew accents show that the word "again" goes with the command that he was to "go," not with the verb "love." The Lord does not call her by her name "Gomer," but the Hebrew word `od, rendered "again" clearly meant no one less than "Gomer."

One day Hosea must have spotted his former wife in the marketplace up for sale on a slave block, naked and exposed in disgrace as a worn-out sex item. She was being offered at the going price of a slave, which was thirty pieces of silver. Surprisingly, the one who would bid on her purchase from the slave's block was none other than Hosea. But why? Hadn't she run off and disgraced their marriage by offering herself to any and every man in that community who wanted to have sex with her? What she was experiencing she fully had coming to her.

But Hosea did not think "it's payback time," or a time for vengeance; he wanted to have his wife back again just as God wants to have his erring children come back to himself again. Hosea did not have thirty pieces of silver, just fifteen shekels. To get the remaining money, he sold a *homer* and a *lethek* of barley (3:2) so he could pay the full slave-price. So, he purchased Gomer and brought her back home again. After the required days of purification (3:4–5), she became his wife once again! What a gracious and loving husband, and what a gracious Lord!

The Application of These Events to Israel

Hosea was told that in a similar manner, Israel would live many days without a king, prince, sacrifice, ephod or even an idol. But sometime after that, the Israelites would return, especially in the last days, and seek the Lord their God and David their king as they would come trembling back to the Lord in the final days of life on this earth.

Outline of the Rest of the Book of Hosea

Hosea went on to deliver the message he had been faithfully giving all during this trying time with the escapades of his wife. The prophet's message was wrapped up in three key charges: God's people had "no truth, no lovingkindness, and no knowledge of God" (Hos. 4:1c). These charges, and the chapters in which they were used for Hosea's message, were:

1. "No knowledge of God": God's people were destroying themselves by a lack of knowledge of his word and of God himself. See 4:2–6:3.

2. "No lovingkindness": God's lovingkindness was like the dew and the mist that evaporated as the sun rose in the sky. See 6:4–11:11.

3. "No truth": God's people loved lies and did not love the truth nor seek to know it. See 11:12–14:9.

Notice how each of the three sections ended in a rosy-tinted prophecy of hope after the Lord's stirring indictments for Israel's sin had been chronicled! Hosea is a powerful story of the persistent love of God for an erring, sinful land Israel and nations that followed in the same path. But it is also a story of how triumphant the love of God was as it exceeded all the sins of humankind! Thanks be to God for such a Savior.

Conclusions

1. Our God will betroth to himself forever all who call upon him in faith believing of his son the Messiah (Hos. 2:13).

2. Hosea and Gomer's three children's names set the background for the ministry of this prophet: Jezreel, the scattered but re-sown people; Lo-Ruhamah, the people not loved; and Lo-Ammi, those who were "not my people"—both of which would also be loved and called his people once again.

3. But these names and actions would be fully reversed in a coming day as those who were known as not my people would become the sons of the living God; those not loved would be dearly loved, just as those who had been scattered would be sown in the land once again.

4. As Hosea paid the price of a slave to redeem his wife, so God has paid the full price for our redemption from the slave block of sin.

5. We today, along with Israel, must place our highest priority of the knowledge of God and his word along with a willingness to show loving-kindness to all and a deep desire to know the truth from God.

Questions for Reflection and Discussion

1. Many commentators claim that agree that God violated his own rules by ordering Hosea to marry a harlot. Do you agree?

2. What is your reaction to God scattering Israel and the Jewish people all over the world and then promising to bring them back again to their old stomping-grounds?

3. Is the current denial and disrespect for the truth an indication that we may be in the last days of history?

4. Do you agree that Hosea did the right thing in remarrying his former wife Gomer after she had publicly disgraced herself in the same town where he was ministering?

5. What made Israel's loving-kindness so fleeting and temporary? How is that so like today's acts of goodness and righteousness?

Lesson 2

JOEL

"Rend your Hearts …
Return to the LORD your God" – (2:12–13)

The book of Joel appears as the second of the twelve Minor Prophets; how his book received this position is not known. We do know, however, that Joel was one of twelve men in the Bible with the same name, which means "Jehovah is God." It is a complete theophoric name: Both parts are made up of two names for God. "Jo" and "El" mean "Jehovah is God," hence "Joel." Beyond this, little else is known about Joel except his otherwise brief background except that his father's name was Pethuel (1:1). We are told from the writer Pseudo-Epiphanius, in his *The Lives of the Prophets*, that Joel was originally from the land belonging to the tribe of Reuben, and that he was buried in Bethmeon, but this seems to be a guess based on 1 Chronicles 5:4, and usually is not taken seriously by scholars.

The date for the ministry and writing of Joel is also difficult to determine, but it seems it either was quite early (i.e., in the ninth century B.C.E.) or quite late (the post-exilic era or later). This study cautiously contends for the earlier date, as the enemies the book mentions are the Philistines, Phoenicians, Egyptians and Edomites. There is no mention of Assyria, which came to power in 760 B.C.E., or Babylon, which rose to power around 606 and was gone by 537.

The strongest argument for the post-exilic date, to explore that option briefly, is that the northern kingdom is nowhere mentioned in the book of Joel; only Judah appears. The authorities, it is contended, also are priests and elders; but no king is mentioned in this book.

It is also most significant that 27 of the 73 total verses in Joel are seen to be parallel with similar words found in many of the other prophets. If Joel did not come first, that would make him a plagiarist of the first order, with almost a third of his book borrowed from the other prophets! So, dating this book is difficult to say the least, but all considered, the early ninth-century date seems the best one for the book.

The Plan of the Book

The focus of Joel is occasioned by the disastrous appearance of an especially severe locust plague, which became the basis for the prophet's repeated call to the nation to respond in repentance before God. The 73 verses are divided up into four chapters in the Hebrew Bible but only three in English translations, which combine chapters 2 and 3 into one chapter.

The Locusts

Biblical Hebrew has 12 terms for distinct types of locusts. Joel uses four: *Gazem, Arbeh, Yeleg* and *Chasil*, meaning "cutting," "swarming," "hopping" and "destroying." Whether these terms are intended in Joel to represent four successive waves of locusts, or four stages in the growth of the same emerging group, is unclear. For Joel, the plague was not evaluated just from its economic impact, but more from its religious significance. Thus, all parts of society were likewise affected and called to repentance. For instance, there was the cutting off of wine to the drunkards (1:10), the failure of the farmer's crops (1:11), the halt to the daily supply for the offerings for the priests (1:9, 13), and even the usually excused bride and bridegroom, who in these unusual circumstances were not exempt from national service, due to the seriousness of the situation (Deut. 24:5; Joel 2:16) as they seemed to be subject to a call-up of what we would label the national guard.

The locusts laid waste to the vines and stripped the bark off the trees (1:7). Everything and anything green were devoured by these critters. Along with the locust plague there came a drought that left the dried-up seed shriveling up under the clods of moisture-less clods of dirt (1:17). As a result, the pastures looked as if they had been burnt over with fire, and the brooks were likewise dried up (1:18–20).

What was an even greater anomaly was that this locust infestation came from the unusual direction—from the northeast. A similar locust plague came upon Israel from the same direction in Israel in 1915 C.E. Some interpreters have tried to metaphorically interpret these locusts, but the descriptions seem too real for that. These insects were "bugging" Israel in a very tangible way!

The Day of the LORD

The theme that links all the book of Joel together is "The Day of the Lord." Even as Joel was lamenting the plague, he announced, "The day of the LORD is upon us." He described it as "great and very frightening" (2:11). In fact, for Joel this "day" was not one single event in the distant future, for it was an event that often was localized, yet it was one the people often faced, while they also shared an early image of what was to come climactically on the last day. It could be both an event of judgment as well as of salvation, depending on how spiritually prepared the people were. Thus, it had both a "now" aspect as well as a "not yet" aspect (see 1 John 3:2). Joel may have been one of the earliest prophets, if not the first, to use this term "Day of the LORD." The phrase is used five times in Joel (1:15; 2:1, 11, 31; 3:14). But it occurs frequently also in the other prophets (e.g., Amos 5:15; Isa. 2:12; 13:6, 9; Zeph. 1:14; Jer. 46:10; Ezek. 30:2; Obad. 15; Zech. 14:1; Mal. 4:5).

The Outpouring of the Holy Spirit and Pentecost

The locust plague, of course, opens the theological problem of theodicy—i.e., how do we justify the ways of God to man? We need to reflect on these passages today against the backdrop of our current batch of massively destructive natural disasters with their accompanying woes and grief, to see how pivotal this book can be for us in our present day. But not only was this to be a day of judgment, it was to be a day of salvation. For example, God would also in that future day "pour out his Holy Spirit" just as he would begin doing on the Day of Pentecost (Joel 2:28; Acts 2).

Repentance

In the face of such national tragedy, the prophet Joel called for a repentance that involved rending or tearing open the hearts of individuals in contrast to the usual mere tearing of one's garments (2:12–13). If God was merciful and forgiving, then it was quite possible that he would relent and stop the crises that the nation was facing, either in a locust infestation or in an invading army (2:1–11).

The depth and intensity of the fury unleashed on Israel with this series of locust plagues was so great that the prophet asked: "Has anything like this ever happened in your days?" (1:2b). This question was not only appropriate for Joel's day, but there are so many things that have happened in today's world that could easily have the same question posted over similar news photos of such horrible events we have seen. For example, what about the 9/11 attacks; Hurricanes Katrina and Sandy; the drought and then flooding in California; and the widespread forest fires, deemed the worst ever known. Have any of us ever seen the likes of such events? Could our Lord be calling us in America through events such as these?

But this is what we are to tell our children so they can rehearse the stories of these tragedies to their children. The events did not happen while God was not watching or temporarily not in charge; he knew all about them and either directed them or permitted them to happen. But for what reason did all this havoc and turmoil occur? What was God's point? Was he trying to say something to a culture that has become tone-deaf to his Word and rebellious to all he has taught? If so, then our Lord has spoken via the events of our day to capture our attention and to turn us from certain destruction that lies up ahead!

Either the tragedy in Joel was one wave after another wave of invading locusts, or one crop of these critters after another that had left the land scrubbed clean of all living vegetation for both mortals and beasts (1:4). This had left every segment of society stripped of its resources: Such a disaster came whether it was the effects it had on the drunkard who was left dry of his wine or his beer (v. 5), the farmers whose crops failed (vv. 10–11), the priests and ministers who were devoid of supplies for presenting gifts at the altar (v. 9), or even about the virgin grieving over the loss of her betrothed (v. 8); the whole country was in shambles and a virtual ruin.

There was only one cure: It was time to gird on sackcloth, the symbol of godly sorrow and repentance, and declare a fast where all would cry out to the Lord (vv. 13–14) in humble seeking after God, and a turning from all sin and unrighteousness. If Joel's audience failed to heed these warning signals, even greater disasters lay ahead of them. What can we today expect considering our sins? Can it be anything less?

Be Warned That the Day of the LORD Is Near – 1:15–20

The incursion of the locust plague was a teaching moment to warn that not only was there was trouble in that day, but to stress the point once again, this would be a symbol or a type of what we could expect in that final Day of the LORD that was just as close at hand. The plague was but a harbinger of the coming day when God would judge all wickedness of a people or a nation that had not been repented of and ceased its sin.

As a result of the plague, an unprecedented drought also happened. The seed rotted under the dry clods of dirt as the granaries fell into rack and ruin (v. 17). The beasts, cattle and herds could find no pastures for grazing, for the fire of the drought and heat of those days had burned them all up (vv. 18–19).

In the plan of God, the issues of wickedness and the iniquity of the nations will especially come to a head at a time known as "the Day of the LORD" or simply as "That Day." This future day was never thought of as a 24-hour period; it was always that sequence of events that was connected to the second coming of our Yeshua the Messiah. At that period, God would bring the historic phase of time and events to a conclusion prior to his thousand-year reign on earth. It might seem as though these days were delayed too long, not only during the days of the prophets, but in our own time as well. However, 2 Peter 3:8–10 warns, "The Lord is not slow in keeping his promises, as some understand slowness. He is patient with [us], not wanting anyone to perish, but everyone to come to repentance." So that day will come; we just do not know when, even though some books claim to know exactly when it will happen.

Thus, according to Joel, the havoc and destruction created by the locusts were but a portent of that great Day of God that was coming. These critters were forerunners of that greater threat that loomed on the horizon. Rather than having the people focus on what they had lost to the locusts, Joel's listeners and readers were instructed instead to focus on the time of enormous destruction that would come from the Lord in that future period. It would exceed anything this locust plague had portended!

Sound the Alarm That the Danger Is Near

Joel used four figures to depict the tragedy the nation faced. It was time to sound off the alarm, for that awful day was quickly approaching (2:1). Thus, the first figure was that of a storm (2:2), for it would bring a day of thick darkness, gloom, and clouds. Joel used four synonyms for this darkness to emphasize its intensity and its impenetrable blackness—the fourth synonym being the same word that described the darkness that befell Egypt in one of her plagues prior to Israel's exodus from Egypt (Exod 10:22). In fact, an incursion of locusts over the land could be so thick that they would blot out the sun and turn the daytime into the darkest cloud and the blackest night one could imagine.

Joel's second synonym was "fires" (2:3): "Before them fire devours, behind them a flame blazes." It is no wonder that the Romans called the locusts "the burners of the land," which is the literal meaning of the word "locust." In fact, a locust can eat twice its own weight in a day. When that is factored in with an infestation of insects amounting to some twenty million tons, that would mean that these critters will consume forty million pounds of green vegetation each day they stayed in the land. The Arabic word for "locust" is *jarad*, meaning "to scrape clean."

A third figure for these locusts was that they had the appearance of horses (2:4). When one gives a blown-up photograph of a locus, it is easy to see how this figure emerged. The fourth and final figure is that of an invading army (2:6–11), which likewise depicted them well.

Joel's vivid figures of the locusts have often been interpreted as a second issue for his audience. Some claim these images were an invading army of men from one of its Near Eastern foes. Others have interpreted these figures as "locusts" that functioned as an invading army in an allegorical sense, a view that was held by the rabbinic commentators and some of the previous interpreters. Others have wanted to see here an allegorical reference to Judah's four great attackers: Babylon, Persia, Greece, and Rome, thus from the standpoint of a ninth-century Joel these were future enemies that would fall on Judah. This is possible, but the meaning of real locusts still fits well too.

Whether the dramatic portrayal in 2:1–11 is of an invasion of conquering army, however, seems to exceed the boundaries of reality. We conclude that there was no second problem of an invading army of men that followed the locust infestation. But even if there was a continuation of the locust description as an announcement of a second problem, like an invading army, it makes little difference to the result. The horror, destruction and havoc rendered by either or both was awesome in its effects, to say the least. It would seem safest to hold, however, that these were literal insects, which on a particular occasion brought God's judgment in a former day on the land in Israel, but they will be but harbingers of the calamitous day of the Lord, which would bring the destruction of the Almighty in a way far exceeding anything seen even in the plague of Joel's time.

Joel was quick to call Israel to turn back to God with all their heart with fasting, weeping and mourning (2:12). It was time for God's people to "Rend [their] heart[s] and not [their] garments" (2:14). The hour was desperate, but it was not hopeless, if God still stood ready to forgive and to show his mercy. The good news Joel had is the same good news we have today: God will change his mind about the forthcoming judgment, even if he had to postpone it to another day when others rebelled against God. Repentance averts judgment—ask the people of Nineveh! Repentance also demonstrates the character of God: He is gracious, compassionate, slow to anger, and abounding in love; he relents from sending calamity when mortals repent and turn to him (2:13). Here, then, in 2:13–14 we find one of the finest explanations for repentance anywhere in the Bible. Indeed, to turn to God with one's whole heart involved a turning of one's entire personality back to the Lord. Such a turning to God involved the will ("fasting"), as well as the emotions ("weeping" and "mourning").

This grace and mercy of God were not to be taken for granted or used as an excuse for not observing a true turning to God. That is why Joel added in 2:14, "Who knows?" Our Lord is always ready to welcome the repentant sinner back into the fold, but that grace must not be toyed with by mortals. It is still up to the Lord to decide how and when to exercise his mercy and love.

Call On the Name of the Lord and Be Saved

Four verbs indicating the Lord's response in 2:18 demonstrate that a radical change had come over Israel as the people repented and the Day of the Lord was for the time being was averted. Correctly interpreted, the text read: "Then the LORD *was jealous* for his land and *took pity* on his people. The LORD *replied* to them and *said…*" (translation and emphasis mine).

A sizable number of the English versions, for some strange reason, render theses four verbs in the future tense, but it is clear in the Hebrew that they were past tense, even though the people's repentance is not explicitly stated as such. However, the results of Joel's preaching were both immediate and temporal. The land was spared further damage from the locusts and the drought because of the people's repentance was lifted.

This may seem strange to some, for how could a spiritual revival also affect the land and ecology? The point is that when Adam and Eve sinned, the dirt and the environment got into trouble because of their sin. In the same way, the Apostle Paul spoke of the ultimate healing of all creation at the second coming of Yeshua (Rom. 8:19–22). The Lord taught this same effect on the environment in Haggai 1:6. The fact that the people of Judah, who were hesitant to rebuild the temple, were planting more but harvesting less, eating more, but enjoying it less, drinking more, but still thirsty, clothing themselves with more clothes, but still were warmed less, and earning more, but still seemingly putting these funds into bags that had holes in them. That, the prophet Haggai taught, was a direct result of their investing themselves in building their own homes, while the house of God lay waste for a total of 16 years, due to an internal dispute over whether it had been the right time to build or not.

But now that the people of Joel's day had repented and turned from their sin, the pastures were now becoming green once again (2:22), the trees were bearing fruit (2:22c), the autumn and spring rains had come on time as it happened in previous times (2:23d) and the threshing floors were filled with grain (2:24) as the vats overflowed with new wine and oil (2:24b). In fact, God would now pay Israel back for the years the locusts had eaten (2:25). Israel must now praise the name of the Lord, for he had worked wonders for them (2:26). All these effects had come because of the immediate response to the national repentance to the Lord—this is what had happened "at the first" (Hebrew *re'shit*; see 2:23).

But there was an even more impressive result, as just mentioned in v. 23, that would come "afterward" (2:28): "at first" there was an initial and immediate divine response to this national repentance on the part of the people. Joel meant by "afterward" retrospectively to the immediate greening of the passages and to point prospectively to what would happen in "the last days," at the end of history. The last days were days of judgment, but also of deliverance. According to Hebrews 1:2, these "last days" had begun when Yeshua came in his first advent preaching that the Kingdom of God had come. Thus, these days will stretch all the way from the time our Lord Yeshua walked on this earth until the conclusion of history.

God would begin this era by pouring out his Holy Spirit, just as he had done at Pentecost (Acts 2:19–20). So effusive would be the gift of the Holy Spirit that it would be likened to something like a tropical "downpour," and not just an ordinary rain-shower. This outpouring of the Spirit would result in the removal of the heart of stone in many Israelites and the replacement of that stone with a "new heart" (Isa. 32:13–15; Jer. 31:31–34; Ezek. 11:16–17, 36:26–28, 37:28–29). This would begin at Pentecost, as an initial installment of that downpour, but its ultimate and complete drenching and fulfillment would await that day when this promise first made to Israel would be realized in the life of the nation Israel in connection with the second coming of the Messiah. The outpouring of the Spirit in all these passages would take place with a priority in the land of Israel itself.

Who then is to receive this outpouring of the Holy Spirit? The Spirit would come upon "all flesh/people" (2:28). This would include Israel's sons, her daughters, her old men, and her young men; in fact, it would also include Israel's men and maidservants—who normally were Gentiles who served them in their homes and work: It would show no partiality either to gender, age, or race! Yes, the promise, Peter taught, was to Israel's children, but it also would be for "all who were afar off," the later expression being a circumlocution for all Gentiles (Acts 2:39; see Eph. 2:13, 17). This is further proven by the fact that it was upon the Gentiles that the Holy Spirit began to be poured out in Cornelius' house when Peter preached his sermon to these Gentiles (Acts 10:45).

In that day, God would also show miracles on earth and in the heavens (2:30–31). This would take place in the awesome and dreadful day of the Lord. However, all who called on the name of the Lord would be saved.

This would also be true of the "remnant/survivors," who were the true people of God living among those who often merely professed to serve and love the Lord, but who truly did not do so (2:32).

Receive the Blessings of God as He Concludes History

If we ask, then, at what point in the history of the world does the day of the Lord arrive, the answer is given in 3:1. It will be at that time when God "restores the fortunes of Judah and Jerusalem." Therefore, Israel's return to her land from the exile and from being scattered all over the earth; this would also be the "day of the Lord," for they were interrelated. The day of the Lord cannot come until there is a massive return and restoration of the Jewish people back to the land God originally promised to them. In this way, Israel is God's prophetic timepiece that would tell us the approximate time on the divine clock.

First, however, a day was still in the offing when God would gather all the nations in the Valley of Jehoshaphat (3:2). There the nations would be put on trial by God for all that they have done to God's people Israel (3:2). Four major reasons are given as why this direct action of God was deserved by the nations:

1. The nations had scattered Israel among the nations (3:2e),

2. The nations had partitioned up the Holy Land (3:2f),

3. The nations had made slaves of the Jewish people (3:3a), and

4. The nations had carried off the sacred vessels from the Temple of God as captured loot (3:5).

The Day of the Lord would center on the Battle of Armageddon, which seemed to begin in the Plain of Jezreel in the north near the town of Megiddo, but it appeared to conclude near Jerusalem in the Kidron Valley, elsewhere called the Valley of Jehoshaphat. The belligerents constituted a large army of the Antichrist, yet the Lord would roar from Zion (3:16). The prophet Zechariah described this same event in his book in 14:1–4, as did the Apostle John on the island of Patmos (Rev. 19:11–16). God would sit to judge all nations as multitudes, yes, multitudes entered the valley of decision. For the moment, the figures of peace in Micah 4:3 and Isaiah 2:4

are reversed as plowshares for the moment are beat into swords and pruning hooks will be made into spears (Joel 3:9–11).

Yeshua described this same day in Matthew 24:29–31. Now that the nations were defeated, Israel's Messianic King could take his throne, and from that point on, he would rule the nations with a rod of iron (Joel 3:17).

There is a blessing phase that follows the judgment phase of the Day of the LORD. The four blessings were:

The healing of the land (3:18),

The obliteration of Israel's enemies (3:19),

The security of the land for all future times (3:20), and

The vindication of Israel as God's chosen people as the Lord comes to dwell in Zion (3:21).

Once again there would come an ecological balance between the physically created order and the spiritual world of belief and trust. Since evil was no longer reigning and had been defeated finally, the physical creation no longer needed to suffer—nor did it! When righteousness reigned, the benefits could be seen in both the physical and spiritual worlds. The mountainsides would flow with streams of new sweet wine and the hills would flow with milk. These were strong figures of speech that witnessed heavy green pasturage of grass that produced the milk that came from the flocks and the vitality of the earth as the mountainsides that provided the right growing environment for the vines that produced volumes of wine (3:18). Water would flow from the Temple area just as Ezekiel 47:1–12; Zechariah 14:8 and Joel 3:18 predicted. There would even come an end to the Arab-Israeli and world conflict between the nations (3:19).

The text of Joel ends with: "The LORD dwells in Zion" (3:21). Israel is back in her land, and the Lord is in her midst.

Conclusions

1. When a correct response is given to the teaching and obedience to the word of God, all of nature and the people of the earth are refreshed. God loves his people enough to also speak to them through the tragedies and havoc of the events of life to get their attention.

2. The call to repent and turn back to God is addressed to us personally and corporately in the nations, organizations, institutions, and churches we each are a part of.

3. The day of the Lord features not only a time of severe judgment on the corporate bodies of people, but it is also a time of deliverance and the promise of the outpouring of the Holy Spirit for all who will turn in faith believing.

4. The time when the Lord will return the second time is closely linked with the enormous ingathering of the Jewish people from all over the world.

5. God will bring all the nations on earth down into the Valley of Jehoshaphat for judgment. His reasons for doing so are spelled out in the text.

6. Four major blessings await the covenant people of God in that final day that include the healing of their land, the obliteration of their enemies, the permanent securing of the land of Israel for the Jewish people and his dwelling in the midst of them.

Questions for Reflection and Discussion

1. What was so special or distinctive about a locust invasion into Israel? Why did God use such a means to highlight his message?

2. Should we today try to assign a divine reason for national tragedy when it strikes us? How can we know if God is trying to speak to us through these modern tragedies or are these just random events that happen all over the world from time to time?

3. What does the outpouring of the Holy Spirit mean and how is it connected to both Pentecost and to the final day?

4. Why is the plan of God so intimately connected with Israel and how is it that God will fulfill his promise even in the face of Israel's monstrous and perpetual disobedience?

5. What is your understanding of the four blessings that come at the end of Joel to Israel and what do they point to in the future?

6. Do you think history will end as described Joel? Why or why not?

Lesson 3

AMOS

Cattleman, Herdsman,
Fruit Farmer, and "Prophet"

The Name and Location of Amos

Amos, whose name means "burden-bearer," was born in the southern kingdom of Judah in a small town called Tekoa. This town was twelve miles southwest of Jerusalem and about six miles south of Bethlehem. The territory of Tekoa, however, extended eastward from the edge of town for some twenty miles down a sloping landscape to the northwestern shores of the Dead Sea. To this day, a modern village survives under a similar name at the elevation of 2700 feet above sea level as a gathering place for several shepherds to water their flocks. But the land slopes downward for some 4000 feet in a tilting grade into the great rift valley, whose great fault line is occupied in part by the Dead Sea.

Even though Amos authored the third book in the "Book of Twelve," he flatly declared he was *not* a prophet, nor a prophet's son (7:14) by profession. This denial meant he was not a full-time prophet, for he was actively and simultaneously engaged in three other agricultural occupations: (1) he was a shepherd, who herded a distinctive type of sheep, so he was known by the Hebrew term *noqedim* (1:1); (2) he was a cattleman (Hebrew *boqer*; 7:14); and (3) he also was a fruit-farmer of fig-mulberry trees, also called "sycamore trees" (7:14). Since this tree did not grow at an elevation above 1000 feet, Amos' grove of sycamores grew somewhere up the slope toward Tekoa, apparently not too far from the Dead Sea.

Though involved in several types of farming, he prophesied too. Amos may have gone on trips up north on occasion to sell some of his produce. Thus, it was when he was on such a trip, away from his farm for one or two weeks, when he also served as a layperson for the Gospel. But as a businessman, he ministered while he was in the northern ten tribes, rather than as a full-fledged or full-time "professional" prophet.

An Encounter with the Priest Amaziah Up North

In an interlude to the message in his book in 7:10–17, Amos related how at the conclusion to the third vision given to him, he had an encounter with the northern priest Amaziah, whose name means "the LORD is strong." Amaziah had informed Jeroboam II, king of the northern ten tribes, that Amos was conspiring against the king right under his nose in the religious center of Bethel. Amaziah further said that by letting Amos preach such words against the north and against Jeroboam, the prophet was provoking a revolution and a sedition against the northern establishment. He had to be stopped by the king, warned Amaziah, for already Amaziah had told Amos, "Get out [of here], you seer! Go back to the land of Judah. Earn your bread there and do your prophesying there!" Amos and his preaching in the northern tribes was unwelcome, according to this priest, for Amaziah deeply resented and totally rejected his efforts at preaching in this northern territory.

Of course, Amaziah had distorted Amos' words as he told Jeroboam; what he alleged was false. Amaziah did this to raise false charges against Amos and get him expelled from their territory. No doubt Amos also was disturbing the kind of teaching that was coming from the priest Amaziah as well. Amaziah had carefully neglected to mention accurately the substance of the charges Amos had raised against the north, or the reason he had raised them. Amos, despite his call for these northerners to repent, had nevertheless held out real hope for the northern ten tribes if they just repented. If they did repent, and make true confession of their sin, then God would immediately have become merciful and gracious to them (5:4, 6). But Amaziah instead insinuated that Amos was prophesying merely to receive payment for his preaching. Yes, Amos had even given these words against the king's sanctuary as well, but he was careful not to aim the words against the Lord's sanctuary! But Amaziah was not interested in seeing the people repent; no, he just wanted to feather his own nest and he wanted to maintain the status quo of the establishment and his situation. These were his people, and he was their priest!

The defense of this prophet back to Amaziah was a very plain and a straightforward response to the illegitimate claims: "I am neither a prophet nor a prophet's son; but I was a shepherd, and I also took care of sycamore trees. But the LORD took me from feeding the flock and said to me, 'Go prophesy to my people Israel'" (7:14). God called him, not money or fame!

Amaziah had defamed Amos' ministry by slamming him with these words: "Do not prophesy against Israel and stop preaching against the house of Isaac" (7:15).

But Amos boldly announced that this was what the Lord told him to say: "Your wife will become a prostitute in the city, and your sons and daughters will fall by the sword. Your land will be measured and divided up, and you yourself will die in a foreign country. And Israel will certainly go into exile, away from their native land" (7:17).

That must have shocked Amaziah as he heard such severe indictments against his wife and children! He would be carted off into exile along with the unrepentant in the ten northern tribes. This, of course, happened very shortly after Amos gave these words from God. Samaria did indeed fall in 721 B.C.E.

However, the northerners regarded Amos as a foreigner, and not one of the sons of Israel, especially under the loud public rejections of his short-term missionary work as a speaker of the word of God as voiced by their priest Amaziah. In fact, Amos dated his speaking as one that had occurred just two years prior to the earthquake (1:1). Earthquakes were not unusual in that part of the world, but this must have been one of epic proportions, for it was used years later as a marker in history—not only to determine the time of Amos' preaching, but also as a marker in the life and ministry of the prophet Zechariah (Zech. 4:4–5). Josephus, the historian, claimed it was this earthquake that took place when King Uzziah of Judah tried to assume the priestly office, which he was not allowed to and was struck by God for his insolence. This event was reported in 2 Chronicles 26:16–23, but there is no factual evidence to back up Josephus' claim about King Uzziah, i.e., that the two events happened on or even about the same time.

The Times of Amos' Ministry in Northern Israel

Amos located the times of his ministry up north, presumably as he went on his selling trips to that part of Israel, during the days of the reign of the Judean King Uzziah (792–740 B.C.E.) and the northern Israelite King Jeroboam II (793–753). This was an era of unprecedented prosperity and wealth in both kingdoms, which unfortunately was accompanied by a mounting crime wave and great social corruption (Amos 2:6–8; 5:11–12).

The Lord sensitized farmer Amos so greatly, by what he saw and what he was experiencing, that he felt these types of moral blight by the people needed to be cared for and preached against immediately. Accordingly, when he visited the northern ten tribes, he saw a people and a land that appeared strong economically but had a deep-down moral disease that was placing these ten tribes in peril, and it would carry them on into the reality of a real collapse of the nation. Moreover, power and wealth were in the hands of a select few while the gap between the rich and the poor was widening every day. Oppression and exploitation were the order of the day.

These social ills widened as the northerners smeared a hypocritical veneer over their religion and then accompanied that religion with a syncretistic adoption of Baal worship along with other gods and goddesses worshiped. Amos scathingly rebuked these religious pretenses; they purported to worship the Lord, but they had mixed in major elements from the Canaanite pantheon, which was not pleasing in the eyes of the God.

Amos' Critique of All Nations Under the Judgment of God

When Amos wrote his book, he dedicated his first two chapters to a stinging indictment of seven neighboring nations, finally zeroing-in as the prime examples of this distorted worship as seen in the nations of Judah and northern Israel (1:3–2:3). He began each of the seven national judgments from God with the introductory formula of "For three sins of [nation], ... even four." This did not mean Amos and the Lord were ambivalent over whether they had in mind just three sins or four, or even a total of seven each! Instead, using the proverbial $x+1$ formula, it meant there were three notable sins, but the fourth and last-named one was the sin that broke the camel's back. Now it was clear that judgment would come.

The list of judged nations began in the far northeast with Damascus. Amos' list of condemned nations then crisscrossed to the far southwest to Gaza of Philistia, then continued then far to the northwest-reaching Tyre of Phoenicia, then crisscrossed the territory back to the nation of Edom, by the southeastern shores of the Dead Sea. Then it moved again slightly north to the Transjordanian and eastern side of the Dead Sea to the country of Ammon, as the divine word of judgment completed his verbal strikes all around Judah and Israel by going a little farther north into Transjordan to the country of Moab, and finally into Judah and the ten northern tribes of Israel.

Perhaps just as the Jewish people in the nations of Judah and Israel were getting comfortable and hoped their sins would not have been detected and mentioned, or perhaps even excused for some unknown reason from God's judgment, the prophet Amos zeroed in on Judah for her sins, but then he really gave a whole litany of sins against Israel as he finished up his list of indictments and judgments, with northern Israel at the heart of the strikes.

Amos' Main Message

Amos then launched into his main message beginning in chapter 3 as he used the attention-getting command, "Hear," echoing the great Hebrew *sh'ma*, repeated so frequently in the worship in the house of God, "*Hear* O Israel that he, the LORD your God, is one" (Deut. 6:4).

After he completed chapters 3, 4 and 5, each beginning with commands to "listen" or to "hear" the word of God, Amos added two sections that warned of coming "*woes*" on the two Jewish nations (beginning at 5:18 and 6:1). Amos ended his prophecy with five visions given to him of what the future held for the people of Israel. But the prominent note of hope was lifted up in the grandest prophecy of all, which was the re-erection of the temple of David in that last day of history (9:11–15).

But it was while giving the fifth and final vision of the five visions that Amos suddenly announced one of the most beautiful promises of what God was going to do in a future day. After the prophet had recited almost nine full chapters containing mostly dreary dirges of judgment, he burst forth with a description of what God would do in that final day of history, and it must have shocked everyone who heard it. Some note how strikingly different this word from God was. These interpreters place these words of blessing elsewhere in Scripture, rather than crediting them to Amos, though no evidence exists to support this assumption.

Even though the northern kingdom of the ten Israelite tribes is as good as gone and forever removed from the list of nations, suddenly Amos started talking about "the hut or booth of David" being raised and restored in its original character and function in the last days (9:11). As Amos put it, this would take place "in that Day," which meant at the end of history in connection with the second coming of the Lord. (7:14–19).

But shortly after this promise was given, that dynasty fell into disrepair and dysfunction. The rightful king of the Jewish nation and the world would come as the legitimate king over all a reunited Israel and the nations of the world.

Most important in understanding this prophecy is the different pronominal suffixes of the three nouns in verse 11c, d, e. It states that "I will repair *their* (third feminine plural) broken places, restore *his* (third masculine singular) ruins, and I will [re]build *her* (third feminine singular) [David's fallen tent] as it used to be" (9:11). The feminine plural suffix referred to an implied antecedent of the two kingdoms of the northern and southern parts of Israel, which God would reunite into one kingdom as a unified nation in that day. The masculine referred to David and his dynasty, which currently was destroyed and reduced to ruins, while the feminine singular referred to the "house" or the dynasty of David. English translations fail to render the pronouns, just rendering each as "it," as if they were neuter pronouns.

Our Lord promised to work on a restoration on "David's fallen *sukkah*, his "tent," "so that he might possess the remnant of Edom" (9:11–12). This would take place "in that day," which would be the final day of history at the Lord's second coming. "Edom" is sometimes used in Scripture to mean all the nations. However, because the consonants are the same, some read *adam* for "Edom," and thus some take Amos to say a different promise. For example, the word "possess" (Heb. *yarash*) was rendered "seek" (*darash*). It is easy to see how the two verbs of might be confused, for in the Old Canaanite script of Hebrew, the difference is only in the length of the downward stroke on the first letter of each verb.

Moreover, Acts 15:16–18 quoted this text from Amos in this way: "That the remnant of men may seek the Lord, even all the Gentiles who bear my name." Interestingly, we now have a Dead Sea Scroll of this part of Amos that supports how James quoted it at the Jerusalem Council, so that reading seems to be the preferred reading.

Conclusions

1. Even though Amos claimed he was more like a farmer than a prophet, he nevertheless spoke the word he received from God to the people in the north, while he was away from his farm, for he was mightily moved by the corruption and sin he saw in northern Israel.

2. Amos gave God's condemnation on each of the nations surrounding Israel and called on all of them to likewise repent, for Israel was to be a light to the nations!

3. Amos began each of his three great sermons in chapters 3, 4 and 5 with the command that the northern Israelites were to "Listen" and "hear" the words God had to say to them.

4. The priest Amaziah tried to drive Amos and his message away from the northern kingdom back down south, to his native land, for he did not like the words of condemnation for their King Jeroboam II, nor did he like his condemnation of their substitute temple and load of sin practiced by the priest and people.

5. Amos ended his words of judgment with a most glorious declaration of the restoration of David's fallen tent/house and its repair so that "the remnant of men [that is, Gentiles] may seek the Lord, even all the Gentiles who bear [God's] name."

Questions for Reflection and Discussion

1. Do you think there was a divine connection between Amos' preaching in northern Israel and the fact that two years after he preached there came an earthquake that would be remembered centuries later?

2. If the formula of "three sins yea four" showed that each of the nations surrounding Israel had sinned to the tipping, or breaking point, what sin was it that finally tipped the scales of judgment in each case?

3. Was there still time to repent and save the northern kingdom when Amos spoke prior to the fall of Samaria and the collapse of the northern kingdom in 721 B.C.E.?

4. What did the restoration of David's house in 9:11–15 have to do with the fact that God was repairing David's fallen *sukkah* so that the remnant of the Gentiles would seek the Lord? Was this part of the Old Testament Promise-Plan of God?

Lesson 4

OBADIAH

"The Kingdom will be the LORD's"
– v. 21c

Obadiah is the smallest book in the Old Testament, a mere twenty-one verses. Like the books of Jonah and Nahum, instead of focusing the message on Israel and Judah, God chose to highlight Obadiah's message for a foreign nation, which in this case was the nation of Edom. However, despite Obadiah's brevity, it has some powerful theological themes, including a discussion of the Day of the Lord, the relationship between God and a foreign nation such as Edom, and God's commitment to his people Israel. Therefore, it would be well to begin by trying to understand the nation of Edom and why our Lord devoted a whole book to this nation, which in many ways was one of the smallest of the foreign nations to come up against the Jewish people.

The Nation and Land of Edom

The name "Edom," meaning "red," seemed to come from an allusion to the "red" vegetable soup Esau's brother Jacob prepared for him in exchange for the transfer of his birthright to his brother (Gen. 25:30). But Edom's name came to be the designation for his descendants (Gen. 32:3; 36:20–21, 30) and to the Edomites collectively (Num. 20:18–21; Amos 1:6, 11; Mal. 1:4).

The land occupied by the Edomites stretched in a southerly direction beginning at the Brook Zered (Wadi el-Hesa) in Transjordania, which ran east just south of the bottom of the Dead Sea and formed the boundary with Moab to its north. The terrain was rugged and mountainous, extending 100 miles south to the Gulf of Aqabah and approximately 40 miles to the east. This territory could be divided into three sections: The first one included a northern section with the cities of Bozrah and Punon (modern Feinan), ranging in elevation from 5000 feet above sea level at Bozrah to almost 5700 near Teman (modern Tawilan). A second area of Edom began at the southern limits of the northern area, distinguished by an escarpment overlooking the Hismeh Valley. This second area extended all the way to the Gulf of Aqabah. The third and last division of the land was west of the depression of land known as the Arabah, the depression that went from the southern end of the Dead Sea all the way south to the Gulf of Aqabah. This area was from time to time occupied by tribes loosely associated with the Edomites (Gen. 36:11–12).

The narrative of how the antagonism between Jacob and Esau developed is one of the foundational stories of the biblical record. Jacob had managed to get his brother Esau his brother Esau as well as stealing the blessing from their father Isaac. Accordingly, Jacob had to flee to Haran, where his mother's relatives lived, to avoid any bloodshed by Esau. Meanwhile in the two or more decades that Jacob was away from home, Esau and his sons had absorbed the original Horite (Hurrian) settlement in the locale just described (Gen. 14:6). The Horites were ruling this country with their own tribal chiefs (Gen. 36:29–30). But Esau took one of the daughters of these chiefs as his wife and thus cemented a close relationship (Gen. 36:2, 25). Then some of Esau's descendants became tribal chiefs among them (Gen. 36:15–19, 40–43; Deut. 2:12, 22). By the time Jacob returned from staying with his Uncle Laban in Haran, Esau was well ensconced in Edom among the Hurrians (Gen. 32:3, 36:6–8; Deut. 2:4–5). Even though there seemed to be a time of forgiveness between the two brothers, as Jacob and Esau met after so long a separation, the whole prophecy of Edom is given over to the bitter denunciation of Israel by Edom and a prediction of Edom's coming destruction.

The Struggle Between the Twins

The book of Obadiah has its roots and origins in the struggle the twins Jacob and Esau experienced in their lifetimes. Genesis 25:23 gives the meaning of the struggle as it seemed to have begun even in Rebekah's womb, where even at an early on time, it had been predicted that the older Esau would serve the younger Jacob.

A fraternal hatred emerged and visibly manifested itself first when Esau resolved to kill Jacob after losing his birthright (Gen. 27:41). That spirit of hatred never seemed to fully dissipate from Esau's descendants; it arose, for example, when Edom revolted against the kingdom of Judah (2 Kings 8:20–22; 2 Chron. 21:8–10). This fulfilled the prediction that their father Isaac had made years prior that Esau would "break loose" from his brother (Gen. 27:40). It is true, of course, that the brothers shared the same practice of circumcision (Gen. 17:9–14) as part of the Abrahamic Covenant. However, the prophet Amos denounced Esau's descendants for rejecting the "covenant of kinship" with Israel (Amos 1:11–12). This anomaly pointed to the reason the Bible repeatedly describes Edom as being so hostile to Israel: It was her violation of the covenant of kinship with Israel.

The Date of the Book of Obadiah

The suggested dates for the book of Obadiah range from a pre-exilic date in the ninth century all the way to an exilic date around the middle of the sixth century B.C.E. and on to even a post-exilic date in the early fifth century. Obadiah itself does not give a date or mention any contemporary kings in Israel or Judah that might assist in dating this book.

The most evidence supports a ninth-century pre-exilic date, but no harm is done if the book was in fact written as late as the fall of Jerusalem. If it is a ninth-century work, as this analysis favors, then it would have been written in either the days of the reign of King Jehoram (852–884) or during the reign of Ahaz (732–716). If the latter is correct, as I contend, then Obadiah is denouncing Edom for revolting against Judah's domination over them, along with for participating in the attacks of the Philistines and Arabs during Jehoram's reign (2 Chron 21:8–17). Note that Amos 1:6–8, 11–12 also mentions the Edomite collusion with the Philistine attackers. The post-exilic date does not seem to work as well because already in the mid-fifth century B.C.E. Malachi speaks of Edom as "a desolation and a desert for jackals." If this were the state of Edom at that time, then the post-exilic date for Obadiah does not work, as Obadiah warned Edom not to gloat over the disaster that had befallen God's people, nor to take part in plundering her or in cutting off any fugitives from Israel (vv. 12–14). A similar argument could be raised against the exilic view: If

Obadiah had witnessed the fall of Jerusalem, he would have written more passionately about it. Admittedly, this too is a subjective argument.

A final argument for the early date of Obadiah is its early placement among the Minor Prophets as the fourth book of the twelve. This is not a conclusive argument, but it is worth noting that Obadiah is grouped with the other pre-exilic prophets, rather than with the exilic and post-exilic prophets later in the twelve-book sequence.

The Author of Obadiah

The name Obadiah is a shortened form of Obadyahu, "servant of God." "Obadiah" derives from the Hebrew participial form meaning "one who serves/worships God." This varies ever so slightly from the Septuagint and Vulgate form of his name, which is closer to "the servant of Jehovah."

Throughout the various time periods the Old Testament covers, there are twelve different persons with the name Obadiah. The most famous was King Ahab's 'Secretary of State' (1 Kings 18:1–15), who went by Obadyahu, and who hid a hundred prophets from the rage and murderous hand of Queen Jezebel. Some think the prophet Obadiah may be the same man who served under King Ahaz and Queen Jezebel, but this is very unlikely.

Names may appear in their longer or shorter forms, as is the case of the prophet Elijah, who has the shorter form "Eliyah" (2 Kings 1:3, 4, 8, 12) and the longer form "Eliyahu" (1 Kings 1:10, 13, 15, 17). The Obadiah of Elijah's day was one who "revered the LORD greatly" (1 Kings 18:3) and who had "revered the LORD from [his] youth" (1 Kings 18:12). Whether these two were the same individual or not is unknown but improbable, as Scripture gives no connection between them.

Edom Will Suffer a Defeat

This prophecy is described in v 1 as a "vision" that God gave to the prophet Obadiah. This word is used to indicate a revelation that comes from God for mortals (Isa 1:1; Lam. 2:9; Ezek. 7:13; Dan. 8:1). False prophets also claimed to receive visions (Jer. 14:14, 23:16), but they did not meet the requirements that defined a true prophet per Deuteronomy 13:1–5; 18:15–23. The visions from God were so closely tied to the true prophets that they were also referred to by a cognate Hebrew term that means "Visioner."

The message Obadiah received was principally about the nation Edom. The prophetic formula was not a throwaway line to be taken lightly, for it marked the words of that announcement as authoritatively and directly from God. Verse 1c could be rendered, "We have heard a report straight from the LORD." The direct speech this text points to was to be delivered by an "envoy" of God. This messenger was sent "to the nations" (1d) with the message: "Let us go against [Edom] for battle" (1e). God, of course, placed himself at the head of the nations in this war against Edom. In Jeremiah 49:14–16, an envoy of God delivers a similar message. Joshua 11:20 says God hardened the hearts of the Canaanites (to match their long-standing intransigence to his call for salvation) so that he might judge them. God does as he pleases in accordance with his righteous character. No one can demand of him, "What are you doing?" (Dan 4:35).

Verse 2 begins what modern analyses of the prophets calls a "covenant lawsuit." It begins with the attention-getting word "Behold" and contains the reason for the attack on Edom, as seen more clearly in Jeremiah 49:15 (Hebrew *Ki*, "because"). God will humiliate Edom by making her "small," and as a result she will be "despised" by all.

Verse 3 notes the consequences that will follow from the judgment rendered in v. 2. Edom will be unable to avert the fate she faced, for despite the pride of her heart, and her abode in the clefts of the rock, she thought all this made her impregnable; but Edom would be overthrown. She dwelt in that difficult mountain terrain that she concluded made her inaccessible, for her capital at Petra was exceedingly difficult for an enemy to penetrate. Since she was perched on such great rugged mountain heights, Edom was proud in her heart and sure of her security. Her mantra became, "Who can bring me down to the ground?" (v. 3d).

In v. 4, Obadiah uses the hyperbole of the loftiness of an eagle's "nest" up in the realm of the stars emphasize how confident the Edomites were in their location. But the Lord made it clear that from those exalted heights he could bring Edom down (v. 4c). He had brought down previous kings and princes, and he could do it again (Isa. 40:23).

Edom inhabited the mountains east of the Arabah, which were made of granite and porphyry. These hills abounded in both natural and artificial caves. Especially noteworthy was their capital of Petra (Sela) in the Wadi Musa, shut in on the eastern and western sides by rocky walls. It was accessible only by a *siq*, a long narrow pass, that could easily be defended from the several hundred feet up the side that towered above it. This passageway would not allow an army to march into the capital in customary spread-out formation, and it was easily defended by a few men, high above, who could roll a boulder or two over the edge of the cliff.

In verses 5–7, the imagery shifts to the darkness of nighttime, when thieves steal and loot. Twice over a rhetorical question completes these metaphors. The word "if" (Hebrew *'im*), with the Hebrew perfect form of the verb, emphasizes a reality that already exists in Obadiah's vision but not yet in reality. The point of the double rhetorical question was that robbers and grape-gatherers normally left behind some of the gleanings of their robbery, but Edom's plunderers would leave nothing.

In verse 6, Edom's enemies will search more intensively. This verse is more fully explained by its Jeremiah 49:10 parallel, where God says, "I will strip Esau bare; I will uncover his hiding places, so that he cannot conceal himself." Thus, Edom will be forsaken and betrayed by all her allies.

Edom was given the national gift of wisdom, but now the Lord would take away all the wise men with the gift of discernment so that God might be able to give them up for destruction (v. 8). The God who gives such gifts of common grace to the wise men of Edom (cf. the book of Job) could also withdraw that gift, which would lead to the nation's destruction. One city in Jeremiah 49:7, Teman, is mentioned as being gifted with wisdom and discernment from God (Obad. 9). This fact is also borne out in the book of Job. One of his comforters, Eliphaz, was from Teman (2:11, 4:1). Teman is mentioned in Genesis 36:11, 15 as being a son of Eliphaz and a grandson of Esau.

Jeremiah 27 sheds light on the use of envoys. Jeremiah sent them back to their respective countries of Edom, Moab, Ammon, Tyre, and Sidon (v. 3) with diplomatic mail for their countries of what God was going to do if there was no repentance in that nation.

In like manner, now that God had removed understanding from Edom's once-gifted wise men, Edom did not comprehend that a breach of her covenant of kinship with God's people Israel would bring his judgment! Such covenant breaking made no sense, but Edom by now lacked the judgment to perceive that she was headed for destruction.

Edom's Crimes Against Judah Itemized

Three pronouncements of guilt are leveled against Edom as part of the violence she committed against Israel. First, God had ordered the Israelites to respect their brother Esau (v. 10; see Deut. 2:4–5; 23:7). Esau was expected to have the same attitude toward Israel. But he instead chose envy and jealousy over Jacob's election and hated him for Jacob's elevation of his brother over himself (Gen. 27:41). Tragically, Esau's descendants chose to continue this same hostility toward Israel, as they later refused to allow Israel to pass through their land when this nation of promise was headed for the promised land God had granted to them (Num. 20:14–21).

In v. 11, the second pronouncement of guilt against Edom is that she did not come to Israel's aid when she, as her brother, had been attacked. There was one special "day" when Edom had acted like a rebellious child. The word "day" is used ten times in vv. 11–14, referring not to a 24-hour period but to the period when Israel was under attack. Thus, what for Israel had been a "day [i.e., time] of distress," became for Edom a day of delight. She gloated, boasted, rejoiced, and participated in the attack on Israel. Any memory of fraternal relationships was summarily forgotten and set aside in favor of the pursuit of personal advantage.

The third pronouncement (v. 12) was tangled up in a complex series of prohibitions. Edom was warned not to gloat over the distress that had befallen her brother, but that caution was ignored. Later in the revelation of Scripture, Jesus would again forbid anger toward a brother, encouraging reconciliation instead (Matt. 5:22–24). The Lord sternly opposed gloating over the misfortunes of another family member; he wanted instead rejoicing when a brother or sister was restored back to the family and to the family of God (Luke 15:11–31). Even if the attacked or fallen person was not a family member, the parable of the Good Samaritan encouraged kind and generous treatment of all people.

Edom is described as going into the gates of the city of God's people Israel (v. 13) and helping themselves to whatever loot they found. Worse still, the Edomites acted as if they were part of the attacking armies, for they "cut off" the fleeing Israelites' escape route and handed them over to the attacker. Edom's covenant of kinship should have taken precedence over any Suzerain vassal-treaty that may have been in place with any other nation, such as was seen in the Hittite Suzerain vassal-treaty. In those kinds of settings, the vassal nation was required by the ruling sovereign nation to capture and hand over all fugitives and escapees from the battle. Edom's involvement and complicity in such actions was just another reason. God would now judge the nation of Edom.

God Will Deliver Zion in the Day of the LORD

With the discussion of all the "days" up to this point in this book now concluded, Obadiah now turns to another "day"— "the Day of the LORD" (v. 15). The prophet Joel had already developed this theme in greater detail, but Obadiah wanted to show it was both a day of judgment on the evil nations as well as a day of salvation for God's own. Thus, this day would mark Edom's doom, but it would also be a day of deliverance and salvation for Israel.

The "Day of the LORD is near" (v. 15), especially for those nations who have mistreated Israel and Edom. Those nations will be requited in kind by the Lord himself (v. 15b–c). In fact, so effective will be this divine requital that for many, it will be as if they had never existed, for God will make the nations drain the dregs of the cup of God's wrath. In Jeremiah 25:15–33, God says the guilty nations will be forced to take the cup and drink "the wine of my wrath," and they will "stagger and go mad because of the sword I will send among them."

This will occur just before Messiah's Kingdom is established. Edom's power be finally and completely be broken, as will the power of all nations who opposed Israel. As all nations gather to fight against Israel in Jerusalem (Zech. 12:1; 14:1), Edom will be among the confederation of nations. As Obadiah taught, "On Mount Zion will be deliverance ... [and] Jacob will possess his inheritance" (v. 17). Israel will no longer be short-changed the possessions she had been promised and that she had seen already as almost complete in the days of Israel's greatest expansion of the monarchy in Canaan. At that time, Israel will occupy those provinces and countries she had been promised and had lost in the interim; "The uncircumcised and defiled [nations] will not enter you again" (Isa 52:1).

The houses of Jacob and Joseph—i.e., the southern two and ten northern tribes of Israel—will now, as reunited kingdoms, enjoy the correction of what had been lost when the unified nation of David and Solomon had split into the northern ten tribes and the two south ones. They would act as a "fire," with Edom being the "stubble" for burning. There is no mention of a remnant of Edom, for all seemed to be "set on fire" and "destroy[ed];" "there will be no survivors from Esau" (v. 18).

As a result of Edom's demise, those who dwell south of Judah in the southern Negev of Israel will appropriate and occupy the mountains of Edom (v. 19a). Similarly, those in the *Shephelah* ("lowlands" or "foothills") of Israel will occupy the Gaza Strip, once held by the Philistines. The tribe of Benjamin, who had the thin sliver of land north of Judah, would also expand eastward into Transjordania in that day to include the land of Gilead in that territory. Moreover, Israel will possess the land to her north as far as Zarephath, which was a town between Sidon and Tyre on the Lebanese coast (v. 20b). Finally, the captives from the town of Sepharad will occupy the towns in the Negev (v. 20c–d). But where is Sepharad? Guesses about its identity include a city in Spain. Jerome thought it was the Bosphorus; others thought it was Sparta; some even likened it to Sardis. Regardless of where these Israelite captives are coming from, together the once separated tribes of northern Israel along with southern Judah and Benjamin will together once more possess the land that bordered ancient Israel and formed separate countries surrounding them. This is a fulfillment of Genesis 28:13–15, where the Lord had promised, "Your descendants will be like the dust of the earth, and you will spread out to the west and to the east, to the north and to the south. … I am with you and will watch over you."

In that final period connected to the events that are part of the second coming of the Lord, "deliverers" will arise in Israel, like the judges God raised up in an earlier era when the book of Judges was written. They will appear on Mount Zion (Jerusalem), and they will govern the mountains of Edom (vv. 21a–b).

In Revelation 11:15, John says, "The kingdom of this world has become the kingdom of our Lord and his Messiah, and he shall reign forever and ever." Similarly, Obadiah's message concludes, "The kingdom shall be the LORD's."

Conclusions

1. The goal of human history is the appearance of the Kingdom of God.

2. First in the events of the coming Kingdom of God is the restoration of his people Israel back into the land of Canaan from all over the globe.

3. Judah and Israel, formerly parted, will now be together once again as history moves in the plan of God toward the fulfillment of his purpose.

4. Edom will be left without a remnant because of their intransigence and refusal to accept the blessing mediated through her fraternal origins in Jacob (Gen. 12:3).

5. The Day of the Lord" is near both in its immediate "now" and "not yet" aspects of fulfillment.

Questions for Reflection and Discussion

1. Esau and his descendants turned the gifts they were given into obstacles to God's grace. What such gifts does Obadiah mention?

2. Considering the Promised extensions of Israel and Judah's territory in the final day of the Lord, can you trace these neighboring territories on a map and estimate by what percentage that will increase the land of Israel? Who will be the losers of territory on that day?

3. How does the "Kingdom of God" fit into this prophecy? What aspects of the actions of God will that include in that day?

4. Where does Edom fit in the present-day geography of the land? How will this prophecy reshape the borders of Israel in the future?

Lesson 5

JONAH

The Angry, Reluctant Prophet

The fifth book of the Minor Prophets is composed mostly of autobiographical elements of his life, but he was authorized to proclaim only eight words of divine revelation to be shared with the people in the capital of Assyria—that is, Nineveh. These eight words were these: "Forty more days and Nineveh will be destroyed" (Jon. 3:4b).

However, Jonah is the only prophet whose career was so atypically but simultaneously and so prominently filled with many miraculous acts of God. He also is the only prophet (outside of Obadiah, which was written mostly to the nation of Edom) whose total writing was addressed exclusively to a foreign people: the Assyrians. Jonah is also the prophet who was mentioned directly by Yeshua in Matthew 12:38–41 and Luke 11:29–32 and whose life was used as a sign of Yeshua's death and resurrection! Here is that sign:

> Then some Pharisees and teachers of the law said to [Yeshua]: "Teacher, we want to see a miraculous sign from you." [Yeshua] answered, "A wicked and adulterous generation asks for a miraculous sign! But none will be given it except the sign of the prophet Jonah. For as Jonah was three days and three nights in the belly of a huge fish, so the Son of Man will be three days and three nights in the heart of the earth. The men of Nineveh will stand up at the judgment with this generation and condemn it, for they repented at the preaching of Jonah, and now one greater than Jonah is here." (Matt 12:38–41)

> As the crowds increased, Yeshua said, "This is a wicked generation; it asks for a miraculous sign, but none will be given it except the sign of Jonah. For as Jonah was a sign to the Ninevites, so also shall the Son of Man be to this generation. ... The men of Nineveh will stand up at the judgment with this generation and will condemn it, for they repented at the preaching of Jonah, and now one greater than Jonah is here." (Luke 11:29–30, 32)

The Man Jonah as a Sign

Jonah's father was named Amittai. He was born in the town of Gath-Hepher, a town in Galilee just a few miles north of Nazareth. We know little about Jonah's life and ministry, but in 2 Kings 14:25 we are given a glimpse of some of his earlier ministry, in addition to this central event in his life found in the book about his ministry at Nineveh after having been the guest of a great fish in the Mediterranean.

In the earlier days of his ministry, during the reign of King Jeroboam II, who ruled in northern Israel, a regime in which this generation was particularly noted for the sins Israel had committed, Jonah was famous for preaching about the restored extension of the boundaries of Israel from Lebo-Hamath to the Sea of the Arabah. This he did "in accordance with the word of the LORD, the God of Israel, spoken through his servant Jonah son of Amittai, the prophet from Gath-Hepher" (2 Kings 14:25). He delighted in sharing this message although nothing more is recorded about this prophet, except the fact that God did call Jonah "his servant" and that he spoke "the word of the LORD" (under protest, to be sure) to the Assyrian people of Nineveh.

It appears, then, that Jonah was far better at preaching about the greatness of the Kingdom of God—especially as Israel expanded her boundaries in Israel and of her victories over Syria. But when he was told to go preach to the pagans at Nineveh, who were constant thorns in the Israelites' side and were infamous for their brutality and violence against Israel, Jonah decided he would have no part in extending God's offer of salvation to such terrorists! He went AWOL as fast as he could.

God's Directive to Jonah to Go Preach at Nineveh

When Jonah was told by God to "go to Nineveh," a city some 500 miles to the east of northern Israel, he decided to go in the opposite direction. That is why he went to the only port-city in Canaan, named Joppa, just south of modern-day Tel Aviv, and there he booked passage for a ship headed to Tarshish, which is perhaps in Spain.

Therefore, Jonah went down to the Israelite coastal town of Joppa, and there he purchased passage on a ship headed for Tarshish. After he boarded the ship, he went below deck and fell into a deep sleep (Hebrew *radam*) as the ship set out on its journey. However, suddenly a furious storm broke out. But Jonah did not notice, for by now he was already fast asleep!

Finally, as the fury of the storm continued to swell, the captain of the ship went down and found Jonah sound asleep, so he quickly woke Jonah and informed him sternly that he had better go up on deck and call on the name of whatever god he worshiped, because their ship was in danger of being swamped and lost by this storm. However, recall that God was still in charge of all that was happening on planet earth, for this storm had been arranged by him to be used for the personal benefit to Jonah.

What Kind of Narrative Is the Book of Jonah?

The narrative in Jonah has been subjected to a lot of debate. The liberal complaint is that there are just too many miracles and too many improbable happenings to make it believable and credible. Therefore, some have tried to get around this so-called problem by claiming this narrative is an "allegory" of a disobedient people who have failed to carry God's message to the Gentile nations of the world. They point to the fact that "Jonah" means "a dove," and that thus, as Israel is occasionally called a "dove" in Scripture (Ps. 74:19; Hos. 7:11, 11:11), this book should be treated as an allegory and not as a historical event!

However, this solution is more imaginative than real. Moreover, this interpretation, even if true, only covers the first part of Jonah's prophecy.

Others have likened this book to a parable, such as that of the Good Samaritan, for in that story of the Good Samaritan ends (Luke 10:36) exactly where the book of Jonah did: with a question (Jon. 4:11). However, unlike Jonah, the Good Samaritan is a story not made up of real characters, with named fathers and characters attached to real cities, such as Joppa or Nineveh. In addition, parables are usually accompanied by interpretations or applications, but Jonah does not exhibit either one of these features.

Others have tried to view the book as a parody or even a satire, wherein the tension is between the obeyed word of God by the pagan sailors and the disobeyed word of God by a reluctant spokesman for God. But that is a stretch of the imagination as well, for even if that were true it would only fit one segment of the whole narrative.

Most conservative interpreters say the central theme of the book is a "historical description" of God's merciful grace and lovingkindness, which usually extends not just to the Jewish population, who carry the Promise-Plan of God, but also to an otherwise violent, godless, and secular culture of unbelieving men and women, even pagan sailors, and brutal conquerors!

But there is an even greater reason this narrative is included in the Bible. The narrative of Jonah being thrown into the sea and living inside a great fish for three days and nights was not intended to be a stray incident, or merely an example of God's special providence as its whole meaning. No, it was put into Scripture to form an essential part of the public character and testimony of the Lord himself, for he later used it to describe his own life and its key events. On two remarkable occasions, our Lord used the narrative of Jonah when he walked here on earth.

Yeshua declared the narrative of Jonah was a "sign," not from this earth, but "from heaven." Moreover, Jonah himself "in his own person" was a sign to those who still could not believe that Yeshua was God come in the flesh. Yeshua was God himself. He had tasted death without going through corruption or decay and had come forth in the newness of resurrected life, and now was one who was showing the path to life, just as the Ninevites had been shown that same path to everlasting life by God's servant Jonah. Just as God had worked in secret in the belly of that huge fish in the lower parts of the earth, so was God working another mystery in the midst of the earth; it would be a sign that would come from heaven. As it was for Jonah, it still was a sign later for Yeshua: a sign of humiliation. Consequently, we can infer that the Ninevites must have asked Jonah how he got to look as he did. He looked strange. And if Jonah said he was put through that period of testing in the belly of a great fish because he had run from God in disobedience, as he claimed, the Ninevites were in just such a similar act of disobedience as he had been on that ship, then was it not possible that God would be merciful to the people of Nineveh, just as he had been merciful to Jonah? How Jonah wished the people of Nineveh would not make that connection, for if they ever once did, then salvation would come to that pagan city, and they would be saved just as he was saved by that great fish! Such a prospect made Jonah unhappy to say the least!

The Experience of the Storm

While the book of Jonah begins in a conventional way with the name of the prophet and his father, from verse 3 on it is anything but conventional for biblical literature on prophecy in the Old Testament. To be sure, Jonah had received a word from the Lord to go preach the message of judgment to Nineveh. But Jonah had no intention of obeying God's directive to preach to his number-one enemies, who were Gentiles.

Instead, he was going to get away as far as he could. Anyway, if the destruction of Nineveh, the capital city of the Assyrians, was only forty days off, and (and he hoped it was), then everything in him yelled 'let her baby, burn,' for that nation had been the bane of Israel's existence. Some may be surprised to learn that God demanded righteous and moral living even from those Gentile nations that were pagan and unbelieving, and that God was watching over those nations just as he was watching over Israel to see how they would act and live. Nothing occurs among the nations of the earth that goes unseen and unrequited by God, for he is completely in charge of everything.

While Jonah was fleeing by ship as fast as he could go, Nineveh meanwhile stood secure and as confident as any similar city of that day could be; after all, she stood on the east bank of the Tigris River, surrounded by walls 100 feet in height and thick as could be, just west and across the river from the modern city of Mosul in northern Iraq. Nineveh was famous for its fine palaces, great libraries, and famous achievements in art, not to mention its wealth and other types of culture. Even though Assyria was terribly notorious for their brutality and violence as well as their urban evil, Nineveh still mattered to God. The Lord was just as concerned for that great Gentile metropolis as he was for any city in Israel or Judah. Nevertheless, Assyria had brutalized so many in Israel, Syria, and other parts of the Middle East, but they never once, at least up to this point, had repented of their wickedness. But now was the time for repentance and the people were convicted by Jonah's message and by the Spirit of God.

Jonah, however, felt himself well hidden from God as he lay sleeping in the belly of that ship as he headed west, whereas God had said to go east! But God in his lovingkindness and grace pursued Jonah by sending "a great wind on the sea" (1:4). So violent was the storm that it threatened to "break up the ship" (1:4b). No doubt the sailors on this ship had seen a lot of terrific storms in their day, but this one topped them all.

The sailors thought it was time to cast lots to find out who was responsible for such a savage storm, for even in their idolatry, they felt such enormous raging of the sea had to relate to the sin of one on that boat. "They cast lots and the lot fell on Jonah" (1:7b). So, they asked Jonah, "Where do you come from?" "What is your country?" "From what people are you?" "Who is responsible for making all this trouble?" (1:8).

Jonah answered, "I am a Hebrew and I worship the LORD, the God of heaven, who made the sea and the land" (1:9).

The sailors were still bewildered, for they asked: "What have you done?" (1:10). Jonah had told them already that he was running from the Lord. Meanwhile, the sea kept getting rougher and more turbulent, so the sailors put the question to Jonah: "What should we do to you to make the sea calm down for us?" (1:11b), for they accepted his story and they felt they had found their culprit. Jonah knew what they should do: They should throw him overboard. "Pick me up and throw me into the sea, and it will become calm. I know that it is my fault that this great storm has come upon you" (1:12). And by now, so did they know the same.

These sailors did not want to be responsible for this man's death, so they gave their rowing one more mighty effort, as they attempted to row back to land once again, but it no use; the storm kept intensifying. So as a last alternative, they lifted Jonah and threw him overboard as he had instructed, when to their astonishment, immediately the raging sea grew calm (1:15). That caught the attention of the men by an even greater surprise, for now they began as one whole crew to fear the Lord and they quickly offered to the Lord and made vows to him (1:16).

As for Jonah, now in the waters of the sea, God provided a great fish to swallow Jonah. Thus, he was inside the fish for three days and three nights, having a "whale of an experience" (1:17).

Jonah Blesses God for Saving Him from Drowning

At first, Jonah must have thought this was the end. And who could swim to land when they were that far? However, God had prepared a great fish to swallow this prophet and to keep him from drowning. This was a huge save for Jonah, and here he stayed for the next three days and nights. Jonah was not wearing a wristwatch, but he used the stereotypical phrase "three days and three nights," which would also be how long Yeshua would be in the grave after he was taken down from the cross. This same expression of "three days and three nights" is used in 1 Samuel 30:12, where an Egyptian slave claimed he had been abandoned by his owners, the Amalekites, as they fled with the captives taken from the city of David, while he was away from his home, assuming he was going to fight with the Philistine armies, armed to fight Israel (see also 2 Kings 20:5; Hos. 6:2; Matt. 12:40, 16:21).

Surprisingly, Jonah's prayer from the belly of the fish was not a prayer for deliverance or escape, but it was a prayer of thanksgiving for his being delivered from drowning. The substance of his prayer included phrases from several key psalms:

"I called to the Lord" (Jon. 2:2; Pss. 18:6; 120:1).

"You [God] hurled me into the depths, into the very heart of the sea" (Jon. 2:3; Ps. 46:2), and "All your waves and breakers swept over me" (Jon. 2:3c; Ps. 42:7b).

"I have been banished from your sight" (Jon. 2:4; Ps. 31:22).

"The engulfing waters threaten me" (Jon. 2:5; Ps. 69:21).

The turning point for Jonah came as the great fish reached the depths of the Mediterranean Sea. Thus, God had been kind to Jonah even though he was trying to get as far away from God as possible. But the Lord was with him, nevertheless.

The word of the Lord commanded the great fish and he promptly burped up Jonah and vomited him up on the dry land (2:10). Thus, God now sends this "spit-up-kid"—his prophet—to head east as he had been originally instructed to go. God gave him a complete "turn around!"

Jonah Is Sent a Second Time to the Ninevites

Now for a second time, God's word came to the prophet Jonah: "Go to the great city of Nineveh and proclaim to it the message I [now] give to you" (3:1). So, off he went on foot some 500 miles east. When he got to Nineveh, he found that the city had a circumference of eight miles, for it was so large that "it took three days to go through it" preaching as he went along the way (3:3b). It is not known if this figure included the suburbs around it or not, for archaeological surveys tell us that the suburbs were spread out in a circle from Nineveh in a circumference of some sixty miles, but it does not appear to include the suburbs.

Jonah arrived in Nineveh and its environs and announced on the authority of God: "Forty more days and Nineveh will be destroyed" (3:4b). There is no record of the possibility that the Ninevites took umbrage to the fact that a Jewish foreigner was announcing such troubling words to them. They may have been so struck by Jonah's blanched appearance from being inside the belly of the great fish and his amazing story of being spit out on the land that they may have thought he had a sort of ghostly aura about him. To them he may have seemed as if he came as if from heaven itself!

However, the text simply says, "The Ninevites believed God" (3:5). The king of Nineveh proclaimed a fast and ordered all that pagan nation, from the greatest to the least, to put on sackcloth—stuff that is about as rough on the skin as modern potato-sacks! The king likewise followed suit as he removed his royal robes and sat down in dust (3:6). The king also decreed that not only men were to be clothed with sackcloth, but so too were the animals, and no one was to taste or eat or drink anything (3:7). The hope was that God would forgive the Ninevites just as he had forgiven the prophet Jonah! I wonder how Jonah was feeling about the success of the word of God. Which would win: his nationalism or his spirituality?

God Shows His Tender Mercies to Angry Jonah

Normally, most prophets would have been pleased to see a whole nation turn back on the Lord, who met them in deep confession of their sins and as he saw their humble clothing of themselves in sackcloth as a sign of repentance. But Jonah was too mad to think straight about anything, much less the great news that the Gentiles had repented almost in a massive revival, for the whole speaking tour of those days had turned out to be just as he had feared they would: Jonah had worried that God would show his mercy to that brutal city of enemies to Israel. Why should they have gotten off so easy just with their repenting and being forgiven? Shouldn't they have paid for all the unspeakable atrocities they had committed in all their military campaigns, especially the ones in Israel? This is why Jonah had declined the call to minister to these pagans in the first place, for he knew that God was gracious and compassionate, slow to anger, abounding in love, a God who would relent from sending calamity to those who deserved it if these people ever repented of their sin and pride! (Exod 34:5). It was one thing if he had been forgiven and had experienced the love of God, for he was an Israelite and a prophet of God to boot, but these forgiven men and women were brutal pagans! "Jonah was enormously displeased and became angry" (4:1). He sulked as he prayed: "LORD, is this not what I said when I was at home?" (4:2). "I knew that you were a gracious and compassionate God, slow to anger and abounding in love, a God who relents from sending calamity" (3:2b). "Now, O LORD, take away my life, for it is better for me to die than to live" (4:3).

God asked Jonah, "Have you any right to be angry?" (4:4).

Jonah did not respond, but instead "went out and sat down at a place on the east side of the city" (4:5), where he made himself a shelter and sat in its shade to see what would happen to the city that he had predicted would fall.

Then the Lord provided a vine and made it grow up over Jonah's head to ease his discomfort from the hot sun (4:6). This made Jonah happy for the moment. But at dawn the next day God also provided a worm that chewed up the vine so the rest of it withered (4:7b). Then God sent a scorching east wind as the sun also bore down on his head (4:8). Once more, Jonah cried out that he wanted to die!

God asked Jonah once more: "Do you have a right to be angry about the vine, though you did not tend it or make it grow?" (4:9). Jonah blurted out, "I do. I am angry enough to die" (4:9b). God's point was that he, the Lord, had made the plants to be used for Jonah's comfort, but as it turned out, these plants, in Jonah's sour-grapes view, were more important than living persons the Lord had also created. Moreover, God had 120,000 children in the city of Nineveh who were not old enough to distinguish between their right hand and their left, not to mention the fact that he had many animals in Nineveh that also needed his mercy (4:10). God had created and nurtured all these creatures as well as all the Ninevites, but Jonah evidenced no sense of mercy or love for these people made in the image of God. So, the story leaves us with a question: "Should I [the LORD] not be concerned about that great city?" *Jonah, what do you say?* End of the narrative, and no response!

Conclusions

1. Jonah is a narrative that comes from real history and real events that happened in the life of a real prophet named Jonah.

2. The prophet Jonah in his person is a "sign" of Yeshua's life in that God brought him back from death with one foot in the grave to life; thus, he was a sign of humiliation.

3. There is a great amount of mercy, kindness, and grace of God shown in this book, including such evidence shown to the sailors on board the ship, to Jonah in the belly of the great fish, to plants and worms, and to the pagan Ninevites.

4. Jonah loved preaching about the expansion of God's kingdom for Israel, but he abhorred preaching judgment when it was likely that if the persons he preached to were likely to repent, for then God would forgive persons who deserved to be roundly judged for their brutality and terrorism! He was a patriot for nationalism, not a prophet for spirituality and revival!

5. God has the same requirements for justice, truth, kindness, and repentance for all nations regardless of who they are or where they are from.

Questions for Reflection and Discussion

1. Does Jonah evidence a case of xenophobia, or is it more a case of wanting to get even with a people who had wreaked havoc on his nation?

2. Do you think the sailors on Jonah's ship really converted or were simply scared for the moment? Did the message of salvation in the Old Testament reach pagans as well?

3. Why did God choose Nineveh as the site for Jonah's preaching? Were there not loads of other pagans between Israel and Nineveh?

4. Does Jonah's use of the language of the Psalms make a modern case for memorizing Scripture?

5. If God had prepared the storm, the great fish, the vine to grow over night over Jonah's head and a worm to devour part of it, does this mean he knew what temper tantrums Jonah would pull in advance?

Lesson 6

MICAH

The Prophet of a Promised
Ruler from Bethlehem

Micah, the sixth book of the 12 minor prophets, came from Moresheth-Gath. The city of Moresheth was in the *Shephelah*, or low-lying hills, south and west of Jerusalem just behind the coastal plains of Israel but bordering the Philistine country to the east of Gaza Strip. Micah is best remembered as the prophet to whom the words about where the birthplace of Yeshua the Messiah was directed: He would be born in "Bethlehem Ephrathah" (Bethlehem) of Judah (Mic. 5:2; Matt. 2:3). Micah's book was mentioned early in the writings of the apocryphal book of Ben Sirach around 180 B.C.E. as being an inspired book of Scripture (Sir. 48:10).

The Times Micah Lived In

Micah, under the inspiration of the Holy Spirit, wrote his book as he ministered in the period of history that saw the reigns of Judean kings Jotham (750–731), Ahaz (735–715) and Hezekiah (715–686), all in the second half of the eighth century B.C.E.—the great century of prophecy in the Old Testament, for fellow prophets also ministered at the same time period as he did: Isaiah, Amos, Hosea and Jonah. Micah also featured not only the telling of the place where Messiah would be born, but also the memorable prophecy that in the glorious future Jerusalem would host the site of Yeshua's future place of teaching his word to all the gathered nations from around the entire world (Mic. 4:1–4) who would receive that teaching.

The Career of the Prophet Micah

The name "Micah" was a common name in Hebrew. It means "Who is like God?" It calls attention to the incomparable greatness and majesty of the Lord. It stressed the fact that no one could compare to him in any way, as his name and character proclaimed, for he superseded any who pretended to be like him. Moreover, Micah, under the inspiration of a revelation from unmatched great God, seems to deliberately have embedded his own name in his own prophecy in 7:18–20, announcing that no one could, or ever did, forgive sin like the Lord! That text reads:

> "Who is a *God like you*, who pardons sin and forgives the transgression of the remnant of his inheritance? You do not stay angry forever but delight to show mercy. You will again have compassion on us; you will tread our sins underfoot and hurl all our iniquities into the depths of the sea. You will be true to Jacob, and show mercy to Abraham, as you pledged to our fathers in the days long ago." (7:18–20, *emphasis mine)*

In fact, these final three verses of the book of Micah's prophecy traditionally are recited at the conclusion to the reading of the book of Jonah on the "Day of Atonement" in most contemporary synagogues. Moreover, at an earlier date, in the same month, the day of *Rosh Hashanah*, the Jewish new year, Orthodox Jews will usually go to a stream or river with flowing water and symbolically hurl in gestures with their hands and arms all last year's sins into the flowing water to be carried far out to the sea and forgotten forever as Micah 7:19 promised.

We do not know how, or exactly when, Micah's career as a prophet began, but since 1:6–7 speaks of a coming downfall of the capital of northern Israel, Samaria, and Micah 6 was addressed to northern Israel, this would mean that Micah's ministry started sometime just before the fall of Samaria in 721. Thus, a date of 735–720 seems about right for his ministry.

In another remarkable reference to Micah and his ministry, the prophet Jeremiah cited him in 26:17–19:

> Some of the elders of the land stepped forward and said to the entire assembly of people, "Micah of Moresheth prophesied in the days of Hezekiah king of Judah. He told all the people of Judah, 'This is what the LORD Almighty says: 'Zion will be plowed like a field, Jerusalem will become a heap of rubble, the temple hill [will be] a mound overgrown with thickets.'"

Moresheth, then, was twenty miles south of Jerusalem in an area described as a no-man's land, because it was so frequently contested by both Israel and Philistia in alternate times in history. But Micah predicted that the city of Jerusalem would be plowed up and left as a heap of rubble, which did happen later.

The Call of a Prophet

Micah does not give us an account of his initial call into the ministry of a prophet as did Isaiah, Jeremiah, Ezekiel, or Amos. But he declared that "the word of the LORD came to him in a vision" (1:1)—in audible tones. Micah, unlike the many false prophets, was not filled self-ambition, self-promotion, or boastful claims, for he affirmed instead: "But as for me, I am filled with power, with the Spirit of the LORD, and with justice and might, to declare to Jacob his transgression, and to Israel his sin" (Mic. 3:8).

All that Micah taught and preached did not originate in his own mind or from his own mouth, but it came from God. He taught with a passion that could be seen by the anguish with which his words came forth as he spoke about the coming judgment of God if the people did not repent (1:9–10). Thus, he gave the message from the Lord with a tender pleading for the return of his people back to the Lord (6:1–8).

Some complain that Micah's messages have a sort of bumpiness or an abruptness, but this effect may be the result of his having pulled together some of his prophesies into a single message, allowing us then to see what he may have said on several occasions.

Micah's Ministry

Micah's prophecy can be arranged into three cycles of judgment, each one ending in a word of great promise and hope for the future. Accordingly, the three divisions of his prophecy would be segmented thus: chapters 1–2, 3–5, and 6–7. Each section *began* with the command "Hear" or "Listen," but each *ended* with a rose-tinted prophecy of salvation and hope that would reverse the tragedies the people were living with at the time.

For example, Micah 1–2 concludes with the Messianic promise found in 2:11–12, while the second prophecy likewise ended in the great words of comfort in 4:1–5:14. The third and concluding section ended with the magnificent words of 7:8–20 and included the supreme words of promise and hope. Most interpreters see a unity to this book and attribute that unity to the authorship of Micah, but some deny Micah is the writer of the whole book. A majority will assign chapters 1–3 to him, except for 2:12–13, while a considerable number will likewise assign the words of hope in chapters 4–5 to others. But that is because they cannot conceive of a writer being responsible for both words of judgment and words of hope. But since both come from the Lord, this distinction does not apply!

The Three Sections of Micah's Promises of Hope

The weary drone of the words of judgment in the first two chapters ended abruptly on a note of deliverance and salvation in 2:12–13. With such a conclusion, Micah suddenly announced that God would one day in the future gather all the sons of Jacob together and bring them together like sheep in a pen, or a flock in a pasture, so that the place of their assembly would one day just throng full of people (2:12). But there would come one who would break open the way of the sheep pen, one who slept in the opening to the pen and guarded its gate as a faithful shepherd. He would be known as "the Breaker," the One who would open the gate's pen; indeed, he would be their "king" who would go before them to lead them to a good pasture. His name is also announced here as "the LORD [who goes] at [your] head" (2:13; see Exod. 13:21. Deut. 1:30, 33; Isa. 52:12). God was not finished with his sinning people Israel; he would not forget his promise-plan to restore them to their land in a grand future day!

The second section of Micah's prophecy came in 3:1–5:15. The rose-tinted prophecies began as early as 4:1–5, a passage important enough to be recorded twice in Scripture (see Isaiah 2:2–4). Thus, if Micah 3 ended with the destruction of Zion, the city of Jerusalem, chapter 4 began with the elevation of Zion as the city that would be exalted higher than any city of any other nation (v. 1). In the predictions in this amazing announcement of what is in store for the world in the future, the nations, often the very ones that had been hostile to Jerusalem, will now instead flow like a stream of water to Jerusalem to be taught there in the Holy Land by the Lord himself (4:2), for he will settle disputes between nations as swords are beaten into plowshares and spears are hammered into pruning hooks (4:3).

Micah went on to describe a peaceful scene where, because of the Lord's reign, all will be able to sit under his own vine or fig tree and enjoy the fruit of their labors (4:4). In that day, the redeemed would "walk in the name of the LORD" (4:5).

In this second section, prophecy began with the triumphal invitation for all the lands and peoples on earth to go up to the mountain of the Lord. Moreover, it went on with the words "In that day" in 4:6, where Micah could speak of the time when the Lord would gather the lame and all the exiles to rule over them from that day and forever more (vv. 6–7). In fact, three titles would be given to restored Judah in that future day: "Tower of the Flock," "Ophel," and "Daughter of Zion" (4:8). Therefore, because the lame and the crippled sheep of the flock will now return home to Jerusalem after being in exile for so long, the promise from God gave great hope. A "Tower of the Flock" is referred to as a place that was about a mile from Bethlehem, which marked the birthplace of David in its fields. Ophel designated the Jebusite stronghold that was adjacent and just south of the Temple area in Jerusalem that David had captured as the site for his capital (2 Chron. 27:3, 33:14), so this title brought to mind the golden years of the reign of David and Solomon; they were a foretaste and a harbinger of what was to come! Likewise, the title "Daughter of Zion" evoked feelings of stability and a beautifully peaceful future of that coming day.

Three more prophecies about the future were recorded, each one beginning with the words "And now" and including the vocative "Daughter of Zion" (4:10, 13; 14), which expressed the concern over the loss of a king and the potential for a long exile. But when these nations come against Israel in that future day, they had better be prepared for the fact that God is still working his purposes for Israel (4:10, 11), for his power is great!

God will restore his people and reestablish, in Bethlehem, David's throne to its former glory (5:2–6). Messiah, the one whose origins go all the way beyond all days, to eternity without end in the past, would be born in Bethlehem, and even though he would be rejected, it was he alone who would come to champion the cause of Israel (5:4–6). In other words, our Lord was eternal in his being!

The third section (chapters 6–7) ends with the magnificent promise found in 7:8–20. This third section had begun with the Lord pressing a court case against his people (6:1–2). It was such a sad time that "a man's enemies are the members of his own household" (7:6d), but despite all the confusion, injustices and outright sinning against the truth of God, Micah declared: "But as for me, I keep watch for the LORD, I wait in hope for God my Savior; my God will hear me" (7:7).

In this glorious promise of hope that follows in 7:8–20, Jerusalem is personified as if she were a prisoner of war who had fallen and was now sitting in darkness (7:8). She pleads with an unnamed enemy not to "gloat over me" (7:8). However, the Lord will come to the rescue of Jerusalem to "plead" her case and "establish [her] right" (7:9). Her enemy may taunt her by asking, "Where is the LORD your God?" (7:10b), but this enemy will soon see the answer to that question when God begins to act (7:10b–13).

God will show his wonders to Israel and the world, just as he did "in the days when [Israel] came out of Egypt" (7:15). Who then can we compare our God to? (7:18). He will have compassion on us, and he will tread all our sins under foot, as he is true to the promises he made to Jacob, Abraham and to the fathers in Israel (7:19–20).

Conclusions

1. Micah was called by God to demonstrate, both in his name and in his message, the incomparable greatness of the Living God.

2. Micah prophesied that Jerusalem would be plowed up as a field and left in heaps of ruins.

3. Micah predicted that Israel's Shepherd would come to gather them as a remnant as the Breaker would open the sheep-pen gate and lead them out into green pasture.

4. Micah predicted Messiah would come to Jerusalem to teach the nations once again.

5. No one could pardon and forgive transgressions like the Lord God, for he would do as he had promised Abraham, Jacob, and the fathers in the covenant he made with Abraham, David, and the New Covenant.

Questions for Reflection and Discussion

1. In what way would the mountain of the Lord's Temple in Jerusalem be established as chief among the nations? (4:1)

2. In what way will God gather all the sons of Jacob and bring together the remnant of Israel? (2:12; 4:6–7)

3. In what way would one born in Bethlehem be ruler over Israel whose origins were of old from eternity? (5:2).

4. What allusion do you think Micah was making when he predicted in 7:17 that the nations "will lick dust like a snake, like creatures that crawl on the ground"?

Lesson 7

NAHUM

"The LORD is Good,
a Refuge in Times of Trouble" – 1:7

Nahum, whose name means "comfort" or "consolation," wrote his prophecy in the seventh century B.C.E., between 650 to 640. His book is placed seventh in the series of the twelve Minor Prophets in the Hebrew, Latin Vulgate, and Syriac Peshitta versions of the Bible, though the Greek Septuagint places it sixth, after Jonah.

The Place of His Residence

Few things are known about Nahum, for his name only appears once in the Old Testament (Nah. 1:1). He is briefly described as a native of Elkosh (1:1), but where is that? Some say it is by the modern village of Al-Qush on the Tigris River in Assyria (present-day Iraq); local tradition says there is a tomb associated with his name. This site is 25 miles north of modern Mosul and just opposite ancient Nineveh, where later in history many Christians resided at that site until just recently. Others, such as Jerome, point to an Elkosh in Galilee, a certain El-Kauze, but no references in Nahum are associated with cities in northern Israel; the Israelites in his book are from Judah. Thus, the same could be said for the suggestion that he came from the town of Capernaum (in Galilee), whose name means "town of Nahum." This suggestion likewise exhibits no history of having changed its name from "Elkosh" to "Capernaum." Finally, some have tried to link it to a site south of Judah called Bir el-Kaus or Elcesei, but there is nothing to substantiate this either. We simply do not know.

The Style and Purpose of the Prophecy

Nahum's book exhibits a beautiful style. As early as 1753, Robert Lowth, the one who first fully described "Hebrew Poetic Parallelism" in biblical poetry, wrote of his deep appreciation for Nahum's writing style:

> None of the minor prophets, however, seem to equal Nahum in boldness, ardour, and sublimity. His prophecy, too, forms a regular and perfect poem; the exordium is not merely magnificent, it is truly majestic; the preparation for the destruction of Nineveh, and the description of its downfall and desolation, are expressed in most vivid colours, and are bold and luminous in the highest degree.

Another, older scholar, S. R. Driver, expresses an identical appreciation, saying that of all the prophets, Nahum was the one who in dignity and force most closely approximated the high style of the prophet Isaiah, for his language was just as picturesque, striking effective in compacting his thought together as Isaiah was. Few would disagree with these assessments, for this description of the fall of Nineveh is one of the best-written and most vividly described collapses of a world empire in the ancient world. One can almost feel like they are personally witnessing the battle being described!

There is also little disagreement on the purpose Nahum had in mind for writing his book: It was to announce the imminent fall of Nineveh and the demise of the Assyrian Empire, which had ruled most of the ancient Near East for almost 250 years. Nahum's challenge was to call Nineveh to repent of their sin, which in this regard was remarkably like the prophecy of Jonah, which also warned the capital of Assyria, a great city of some 300,000, and of a similar pending earlier destruction and collapse of the city and empire within forty days if they did not repent.

However, there was one dramatic difference: The people of Nineveh on Jonah's day repented of their evil a little more than a century earlier. But in Nahum's day, they refused to do so. They mocked the prophet's call to repent by saying, in effect, "We have heard this kind of talk around here once before. Over a century ago we were told by a Jewish prophet named Jonah to repent, or the city and empire would be destroyed, but nothing like that ever happened. We are not going to fall for that twice!" … Or so their responses might have gone!

One thing remained true: God was sovereign over all the nations, not just Israel and Judah, so whenever one of these nations decided it could be as oppressive and ruthless as it wanted, there was always the Lord God they had to face for their savagery—either in judgment in the here-

and-now on earth, or in that final day when Messiah returned. Nahum brings two abiding principles of the Lord into one single prophecy: his judgment and his mercy. It would indeed be judgment for Assyria, but mercy for Israel.

The Date of the Prophecy of Nahum

As for the date of this prophecy, it can best be determined by noting its allusion in 3:8–10, which refers to the Assyrian conquest of that world-class city of that day, Thebes, in 664–663 B.C.E. Nahum thus predicted the fall of Nineveh, Assyria's capital, which did come in 611–612. Accordingly, this prophecy of Nahum must have been written sometime between 663 and 612. No Judean king is named in this book. Had King Josiah (640–609) been reigning, it is doubtful anyone would have hesitated to put his name down in this book. But it seemed more likely that wicked King Manasseh (686–642) was king when Nahum wrote down his message from God. Who would want to associate Manasseh's name with the mercy of God toward Judah during the evil that the king perpetrated?

Hymn to the Vengeance and Goodness of God

Nahum gets right to the point of his ministry. He wants to make a point; one he sees as the central focus of his book: No one less than the King over all mortals and things is the Lord of the universe. And this Lord God is exceedingly angry with his enemies (1:2). Nahum paints God's character as very zealous and jealous for his name's sake and for his cause; in fact, he will take vengeance on all who by their sin dishonor his name, for all sin is simultaneously an assault on God's holiness and a defilement of all he is and all he stands for. Even though the Lord may withhold his wrath for a long time, since he is slow to anger, still "he will not leave the guilty unpunished" (v. 3b). He has set a time when he will judge the sins of the wicked (2 Pet. 2:9).

What follows is a mighty description of God's power and majesty as seen in his wrath, and in his mastery over the forces of nature (vv. 3c–6). It was this same disclosure of his person that had been demonstrated years earlier in his deliverance of Israel from Egypt, which is celebrated not only in this text (v. 4) but throughout the Scriptures. Who then can stand before his indignation, which is so deeply aroused by sin? If God can rebuke the oceans and the seas, or make mountains shake violently at his approach, so that the hills melt in his presence, how can mortals presume that they will avoid the fury of his wrath in the face of their persistent wickedness?

Accordingly, mighty Nineveh must face up to the fact that she must give an account for all the savagery she has committed! If Nineveh—or any nation—thinks their chariots, horsemen, walls, generals, or technicians can avert God's judgment, they are very wrong. The emphasis is on the "vengeance" of God, a word that appears three times in the participial form in v 2, from the Hebrew root *naqam*; this is an ongoing, yet-completed process. This, then, is a warning not to take God lightly. However, God's vengeance will not suddenly flare up and boil over like human wrath, as if God might suddenly lose his temper. Verse 3a taught: "The LORD is slow to anger and great in power, [yet he] will not acquit the wicked." Nor will he ever get distracted and forget about the judgment that awaits a continually sinful nation such as Assyria. Punishment will come to those who deserve it. Not only is God the God of love, but he also is a warrior, who rides the mighty storm clouds as his war chariot into the scene of battle (Pss 18:8–16; 68:5–7; Matt. 24:30).

God's power and greatness can be seen not only in the drying up of the Red Sea and the Jordan River at a word from his servants, but also in reducing the legendary beauty of the pastures of "Bashan," "Carmel" and "Lebanon" to nothing but dried-up fields (v. 4c; Mic. 7:14). One word from God's lips, and these spots will become stubble and dust. This word was not only addressed to Nineveh but also to Assur and all of Assyria—in fact, "the world and all who live in it" (v. 5c). No person or land is outside the sphere of God's divine sovereignty or wrath if it is needed. It is time for the people of Nineveh to repent, as they had in Jonah's day. But that was not going to happen in the seventh century—or so it seems!

Suddenly this hymn in chapter 1 turns to another song, about God's goodness (v. 7). This juxtaposition of both God's judgment and his grace, mercy and goodness in the same message is foreign to many scholars, who feel that a writer should choose one thing or the other, not both wrath and love, judgment, and restoration, in the same writing! But Nahum, writing for different people and for distinct reasons, includes both aspects of

God's nature. God is the source and the essence of goodness (Luke 18:19), for in times of trouble, he is our "refuge/stronghold" (v. 7b). So rather than relying on fortified walls for protection, the Assyrians should have turned to God himself as the best stronghold to take refuge in, for he "cares for those who trust him" (v. 7c). The same offer of salvation and deliverance was opened beyond Israel to Gentiles.

But if Nineveh was going to trust in God, the sin question had to be dealt with first. God's goodness did not eclipse and wash over his concern for the wickedness this nation had committed. God would not leave them unpunished (v. 3b); this violence had to be confronted, and forgiveness had to be requested.

Since Nineveh's sin went unconfessed and thus unforgiven, God would bring an "overwhelming flood" (v. 8). This brought an end to that city, as Nahum had predicted. It would have been far better for Assyria to have repented as the people of Nineveh had done in Jonah's day. God's name, honor, power, severity, and goodness would all have been vindicated, no matter which way the people decided to go.

Judah Safe at Last

Nahum turned now to address Judah with an assurance that he would personally deliver them (1:12–15). The message of good news begins with the only example of the prophetic-messenger formula in the whole book: "This is what the LORD says" (1:12). Immediately the prophet brings together the previous message of judgment for Assyria with his message of salvation for the people of God (later identified as "Judah" in v. 13d). The northern ten tribes had been taken into captivity by the Assyrians in 722 (2 Kings 17), but for the last half of the eighth century and the first part of the seventh century, Assyria had reduced Judah to little more than a puppet government burdened and subjected to heavy tribute and taxes.

Though Assyria felt safe and relied on the fact that they "were numerous," nothing would save them (v. 12). Neither friends nor numbers would help Assyria avoid God, for they would be "cut down." This is the same Hebrew word used for shearing fleece. Indeed, that is what had happened to Assyria in 701, when King Sennacherib sent Rabshakeh, his top officer, to demand the Judean king Hezekiah should no longer resist his armies but instead immediately surrender to the Assyrian siege set up against Jerusalem, for no god of any other nation had ever delivered their country out of Sennacherib's hands. What did Hezekiah and the people of Judah think the Lord their God could do for them? Cocky Sennacherib and Rabshakeh got the answer quickly. God delivered Hezekiah out of their Assyrian hands; on that very night 185,000 Assyrian troops mysteriously and suddenly died (2 Kings 18:17–19:37), and the monarch beat it home as fast as he could. He thought on the way home, *I should never have messed with Jehovah at all. Should not have authorized those blasphemous speeches against the Lord, either.*

In this manner, God "broke the yoke" (1:13a) that had "afflicted" Judah for so long. And so, the suffering that had stretched over Judah for decades from the harsh treatment of Assyria was over, and it would be "no more" (1:12e). In another pronouncement, God said the king of Assyria would have no heirs to succeed him, his cultic images in his Temple would be destroyed, and Sennacherib would die and be buried (v. 14).

On the other side of the picture was verse 15, which sounded forth a similar message to Isaiah 52:7 and Romans 10:15. Shifting away from the message of Assyria's fate, verse 15 began suddenly with "Behold." A herald was spotted running on the mountains, from the battle lines with news from the front to those back home—news that in this case turned out to be beautiful, proclaiming "peace."

Nineveh Is Literally "Washed Away"

The Assyrians' reputation for violence was known among the nations of the ancient Near East. Now God would raise up "he who scatters," from "an attacker" (see 2 Sam. 22:15; Ps. 18:14.; Isa. 24:1) who would advance toward Nineveh. This interpretation is made clear by the way this section concludes: "Behold, I am against you, says the LORD of Hosts." God had had enough of the atrocities, evil and wickedness, so he finally intervened.

Originally, Nineveh had been attacked in 614 B.C.E. by Cyaxerxes (ca. 625–585), king of the Medes, but he was only able to take a section of the suburbs of Nineveh, not the capital city itself. He teamed up with the Babylonian King Nabopolassar and Umman Manda (possibly Scythian), and together they brought down Nineveh in 611–612.

Nahum let loose with a series of biting commands in short, staccato military fashion, as if they had come from the lips of a frightened but exhausted leader who was suddenly involved in a final stand: "Man the fort! Watch the road! Brace yourselves! Marshal all your strength!" (2:1)

But it was too late. The armies attacking Nineveh were already in place; it was too late to prepare for the attack on this capital city. Since Nahum had foretold the complete destruction of Nineveh in chapter 1, he now moved on to the grim details of how so great a city went extinct.

The Lord would suddenly step in against Nineveh as he avenged Judah for all they had suffered; Nineveh may have plundered the people of God in previous days, but now new plunderers would loot the city of the old plunderers' unprecedented wealth (2:2). In the past, Nineveh had repeatedly ruined the vine of Israel as it robbed her of her fruit, cut off her branches and left only the main stem remaining (2:2d), but those days were over.

With obvious drama and a sense of the swift action taken against Nineveh, verses 3–4 depict the shields, the uniforms of the attackers, the speed of the chariots, and the flashes of light bouncing off the ensuing battle equipment. We are not sure what was "red" in this entourage; it may have been the scarlet of their military uniforms. It may even have been the reddish color of the Cyprus-wood spears. But the scene was a wild one, for the charging chariots of the attacker careened madly in the streets, spreading terror and death wherever they went.

The attack on Nineveh moved from the streets of the city's suburbs to the central city of Nineveh itself (v. 5). So vast was the number of attackers that they stumbled and fell over each other as they hastened to man the wall of Nineveh. Now that the besiegers were at the wall of the city, Nahum devoted the rest of his time to telling how the city would be captured, its spoils taken, and the desolation left (v. 6). The city would fall as "the river gates are thrown open" (v. 6a). One of three neighboring rivers, the Tebiltu, originally flowed through the heart of the city. The Khosr was formed into a reservoir outside the city at some distance, with two massive walls holding back the waters. But Nahum depicts that the double dam walls were opened by the enemy, and the gate where the Khosr entered the city along with the adjoining wall, was destroyed by a sudden massive flood of water. With this tidal wave sweeping into the city, the palace collapsed (v. 6b).

Attention shifts to the woman or women of the palace in verse 7. It is not possible to translate the Hebrew word *Huzzah* with certainly. It is usually rendered "stripped," and the verse may refer to the Assyrian queen herself, or more likely, it may figuratively refer to the city itself.

That Nineveh is described as "a pool whose water is draining" (v. 8) again points to the inundation that came upon Nineveh brought on by her attackers; the city had been flooded, its palace walls were teetering on the edge of collapse from the floodwaters, so the city looked like a pool.

With conditions so devastating and the people fleeing as fast as they could, Nahum poetically orders the conquerors, "Plunder the silver! Plunder the gold! The supply is endless" (v. 9). Verse 10 surveys the crushed city. Nahum uses a bit of wordplay with the words *buqah, umebbuqah, umebbullaqah* ("desolation, devastation, dilapidation"). This once-proud city lay in ruins after also being thoroughly plundered. Nahum breaks off his description of the devastation of Nineveh to lift his own taunt-song with Assyria as a place where "lions" lived (v. 11). Assyrian kings loved to depict themselves as lions. In verses 11–12, Nahum mockingly asks where the riches are that the lion of Assyria previously plundered violently from other nations. Verse 12 likewise asks where is the lion that once enriched Assyria by tearing apart other nations. Assyria's cruelty and brutality was unparalleled. This is why Jonah had been so reluctant to preach to such violent men and women; he did not think such people deserved a chance to repent. Verse 13 wraps up the theme of the whole book when the prophet declares in the name of the Lord of Hosts that God himself was against Assyria. Nineveh must be wiped off the face of the earth, according to God's sure word. Having had enough, he stated plainly, "I am against you" (2:13; 3:5), a judgment repeated often in other prophets (Jer. 21:13; 23:30–31; 50:31; 5:8; 13:8, 20; 21:8; 26:3; 28:22; 39:1). This is why God would "burn [Nineveh's] chariots, the Assyrian's prized weapon of war, devour the military with the sword, stop Nineveh's carnage and put an end to all those haughty messengers and heralds of the king that spoke against all others, even God himself (v. 13).

Woe to the City of Nineveh

The drama of the battle scene of Nahum 2 is followed by a song that weaves together a taunt and some mockery. The end of Nineveh is near, so a "woe" is pronounced against her by the Lord, as was usually expressed over those who were doomed by God with sure destruction (Isa. 5:8–24; 10:1–3; Mic. 2:1–4; Amos 5:18–20; 6:1–7, etc.). Nineveh was called "the bloody city" (3:1), because of its cruelty to and oppression of the nations it victimized. The Assyrians were brutal beyond words.

Some of the drama of the battle scene found in 2:3–10 is resumed in chapter 3. So graphic and detailed is Nahum's description of the overthrow of Nineveh that many declare the vividness unexcelled in sacred or secular literature. One can almost hear the crack of the whip, the noise of the chariot wheels over the rough stones, the horses rearing up and snorting, the flashing of the swords, the jumping of the wagon wheels over the piles of corpses, and the implements of war now abandoned and littering the landscape like a junkyard. No wonder God repeated the charge: "Behold, I am against you says the LORD of Hosts" (2:13, 3:5).

But Nineveh was guilty also of a "multitude of whoredoms" (3:4). Like so many other nations, Nineveh was "the mistress of witchcraft" (v. 4b), for she used her sorcery seduce and overcome other nations as they tried to learn the fate of those she attacked and the outcome of her own military future. But God's reaction to all who used any form of the occult was clear: "Anyone who does these things is detestable to the LORD; because of these same detestable practices, the LORD your God will drive out those nations before you" (Deut. 18:12). Accordingly, God forbade all these ways of avoiding his revelation for any of his people, or for any other nation, which included divination, astrology, going to an enchanter, a sorcerer, a necromancer, or a clairvoyant. This warning was not only found in the Old Testament (Deut. 18:9–14), but also in the New Testament (Gal. 5:19–21).

Nineveh, once an imperial power that lorded over the nations she had subdued, would now be exposed as a harlot, with filth cast at her as she became the spectacle for all the world to see (3:5–7). Five times the first-person "I" is used in vv. 5–7, emphasizing God's personal intervention against Assyria. It is represented as a woman whom God will "uncover

[her] skirts over her face," showing the nations her nakedness. In fact, Nineveh will be just as vulnerable as Thebes would have been. Thebes had allies, but Nineveh had none. So, this was the question for Nineveh: "Are you better than Thebes, that was situated on the Nile?" (v. 8). This same haunting question should be asked of all world capitals that think they are too big to bow down before the God of gods and Lord of lords.

Two Taunt-Songs for Defeated Assyria

Nahum's prophecy began with a song that exalted God's character and ability to avenge evil, but now in 3:14–19, this prophecy ends with two taunt-songs that show that evil will be overcome.

With heaps of ironic imperatives, the prophet directs Nineveh to get ready for a siege. It could do this best by storing up water in its cisterns in the city, for they would need that water to make replacement bricks to repair the portions of the wall as the attackers and flood felled them (v. 14). A fire will break out in the city, which will consume them as the enemy's sword cuts them down (v. 15). Nineveh can heap up its defenders as prolifically as swarms of locusts (v. 15d), but it will do no good; God has decreed their end. Nineveh had great wealth, but possessions mean nothing to God (vv. 16–17); they will be gone like a swarm of locusts that suddenly leave.

Nahum 3:18–19 is really a dirge; this once-proud city, with "shepherds" (military commanders) and nobles, are now corpses scattered all over the mountains. There is not even one to gather up the bones (v. 18). Finally, all who hear the of Nineveh's fall are clapping with a vengeful joy that she has finally gotten what she deserved. No one mourns Nineveh's fall; it comes as a huge relief after two centuries of brutality and violence. Nahum ends with the words, "Who has not felt your endless cruelty?" (v. 19c).

Conclusions

1. Nineveh goes a long way toward proving that "righteousness exalts a nation, but sin in a reproach to any people" (Prov. 14:34).

2. When wickedness reigns with no regard for persons or God's teaching, it is bound to face his judgment, both now and in the future.

3. The Lord is slow to show his anger and to deal with unrighteousness, for he wants all to have an opportunity to come to repentance. But his zeal for his name and his holiness will mean that we can be sure that he will act at the proper moment.

4. We can also be sure that he will not allow his people to use magic to try to find out what the future holds. This is why there is such a strong denunciation of ways of consulting witches, necromancers, mediums, and the like instead of going to God's word. He clearly denounced these things in Deuteronomy 18:9–14. No believer should dabble in any cultic practice.

Questions for Reflection and Discussion

1. Why do you think God allowed Assyria to practice such brutal methods of warfare all over the ancient Near East for some 250 years before finally intervening? Were there any warnings to Assyria along the way? Did she ever show repentance for her deeds?

2. How do you reconcile God's jealousy/zealousness with his love and desire that all would come to repentance? Can these two attributes be harmonized? How?

3. Why is 1:7 ("The LORD is good, a refuge in times of trouble") placed right amid his declaration that he will take vengeance on all unrighteousness?

4. How can God place so many songs in a part of the Bible that has so awesome a group of warnings about his impending wrath?

5. Some descriptions of God's vengeance are quite graphic. How can we reconcile the descriptions of God as "good" with those of him as being an avenging God?

Lesson 8

HABAKKUK

"The Just shall Live by Faith" – 2:4c

Habakkuk, the eighth book of the twelve Minor Prophets, is best known for his central assertion, "The just shall live by faith" (2:4). It is especially significant because it is also repeated three times in the New Testament (Rom. 1:17; Gal. 3:11; Heb. 10:38). But the book had its genesis somewhere just before 600 B.C.E. in an impassioned argument between the Lord and Habakkuk. This prophet was filled with a load of frustration and many questions over the corruption and sin he had seen all around him in the land of Judah. His frustration was over both individual and corporate sin. Moreover, his concern could be narrowed down to this question: Why wasn't God doing something about such an overwhelming persistence for sinning amongst the people of Judah? So, in a way, this book begins with a theodicy, a desire to justify the ways of God with the ways of humans. But Habakkuk's frustrations did not lead him, as happens so often today, to go on a rampage of mindlessly smashing store windows, looting merchandise, setting vehicles on fire, shooting a bunch of people before taking his own life; no, his method of expressing his frustration was altogether different from how our present-day culture tends to express its desire to call things dramatically to the public's attention.

However, frustration is a key word that certainly describes the prophet's concerns and our own current anxieties; but the current frustration tends to be more of a corporate and communal type: frustration over racial injustice, employment injustices, the presence and injustice of international wars, and so forth. In contrast, however, our generation seldom pauses to express frustration over own personal sin; no, it is all about "them" and what "they" are doing to "us." Nevertheless, life itself is full of frustrations without adding national and international concerns to our list.

In recent history we have seen massive destruction of life and property in situations that did not appear to be just in the eyes of the perpetrators. To call public attention to these failures, often those who felt offended in our day would go on a rampage of burning, killing, and destruction. But how did that help answer or assuage the problem? True, life is full of frustrations. But how each of us faces these problems is a whole other matter. Here is where the book of Habakkuk comes in. So, we go to his book for answers to the prophet's concerns as well as to find answers to some of our own current problems and how we can react to them as we should.

The Author of Habakkuk

Other than what is in the introduction, we know nothing else about the author of this book. He was God's messenger to Judah. His name may come from *hambaququ*, Akkadian for an herb, or from the Hebrew verb *habaq*, "to embrace." He was sent to this Jewish nation to warn them about the imminent invasion of the coming attack by the Babylonians (a.k.a. the Chaldeans), whom God would send as the agents of his judgment for the same grievances Habakkuk had noticed among the people of Judah. The Lord and his prophet faced much the same situation we face today, even though America partially claims to have been at one time a godly nation. Americans, like the people of Judah, claimed to believe in God generally, yet there was a high incidence of violence, with an increasing number of homicides each year, an enormous escalation in the number of separations and divorces, a huge number of abandonments of children, an inordinate number of deaths on the highways from drunk drivers, not to mention a ton of other injustices in the courts of our times now facing the government. Where during all of this was God? Surely God was aware of these situations, so why were they allowed to continue? Wasn't he powerful enough to manifest himself in types of dramatic action?

The word God gave to Habakkuk opened his book by calling it a "burden" (Heb. *massa'*). This word occurs 39 times and usually refers to a "load" or a "burden" on the back of animals. But in prophetic speech it appears 27 times in speeches that are threatening or of a minatory character. The contents of these prophecies, then, consists exclusively of

76

threats from God and thus should be rendered a "burden," not merely an "oracle" or mere "prophecy" as many translations improperly prefer today.

The Prophet's Frustrations

More than a half century before the time of the first coming of Yeshua, Habakkuk cried out, "How long, LORD, must I call for help, but you do not listen? Or cry out to you, 'Violence!' but you do not save?" (Hab. 1:2).

The increase and persistence of evil never seemed to end or to find a just answer from those in charge. There was violence, strife, contention, destruction, lawlessness, injustice, and impiety everywhere (1:3–4). Worse still, God, the government and the priests were doing nothing about it! Habakkuk would preach, but there seemed to be no visible results among the people of Judah. God was letting the people get away with everything. What was this world coming to?

True, Habakkuk had put his concerns in the form of a lament-prayer, which was a standard form for crying out to God for relief when one was in despair in that day. Moreover, since we are told that Habakkuk had some sort of Levitical background (3:1, 19), this book may also represent an intercessory prayer on behalf of the people of Judah. Intercessory prayer was one of the key functions of a prophet's calling and task. A prophet prayed not only for himself, but his was the responsibility to pray for the nation and to stand in the gap as a mediator between God and people.

The effect of the chaos that ensued was that "the law is paralyzed" (1:4a). But the order that God had ordained was called "justice" (Heb. *mishpat*, 1:4). The people of Judah, under the kingship of Jehoiakim (609–598), had jettisoned God's way of righteousness in exchange for their own—the exact opposite of what God had ordered for society. Still, many of these same people had recently affirmed during the revival that had come under King Josiah, 15 to 20 years prior to Habakkuk's prayer, much that was the opposite to their current practice! Justice would be established if God's people would only pay attention to God *torah*—his teaching, his instruction." But when his instructions are abandoned, the result for society is chaos.

What was Habakkuk to do? He was confronted with evil on every hand. There were a few righteous people, but they were not even making a dent in the wickedness. Added to all these troubles was the prophet's perplexity of unanswered prayer (1:2). But suddenly there came an answer from God.

The Lord Answers Habakkuk

Habakkuk got the answer to his lament, all right, but it was not at all what he was expecting! It left him stunned and ready to ask a whole lot more questions. But first, the Lord informed his servant that he was not at all ignorant or indifferent to the chaos and the accumulated sin his people had created. God would shortly intervene with his judgment against Judah. But how would God work? He would do something that few would believe even if it had told them at that very moment (1:5b–c).

God would "raise up" the "Babylonians" (1:6a), brutal conquerors known for their "ruthlessness and impetuosity," invaders who would "sweep across the whole earth to seize dwellings not their own," a "feared and dreaded people," who were "a law to themselves and [who] promote their own honor" (1:6b–7). Even so, they still were under the oversight of the Lord, and they were directed to accomplish God's purposes for his glory. All this must have shocked Habakkuk and all who heard it. Wow! Why would God use a bunch of militaristic thugs like this nation? Judah was bad and wicked, yes, but these brutes were far worse than any of them! How could anyone reconcile such differences in the planned action of God?

The implications of such an announcement of divine judgment, with its use of such agents of punishment, who were admittedly more wicked than Judah, was a staggering and stunning message. It pointed to the fact that the presence of turmoil, violence, and death in that day (as well as our own) was troubling enough. But what can we say about God's permitting this turmoil to go on? Might it be evidence not of God's absence but of his working his purposes for his glory? God will always be Lord of history and he will always work, even though that work may at first be frightening, mystifying, and alarming to the *nth* degree.

The Babylonians made a virtue out of violence, for their horses were as agile and swift as leopards (v. 8a). They were greedier than wolves at dusk pursuing their prey (v. 8b), and their thirst for the battlefront and war made them as ravenous as circling vultures or eagles (v. 8d). The unjust

Judeans would now be treated unjustly by the unprincipled pagan Babylonians (1:9). Both Jeremiah and Ezekiel refer to the fact that the Chaldeans were skilled horsemen and their horses were extremely swift and battle-hardened (Jer 4:13; Ezek. 23:23). This is the exact picture Moses had drawn for the nations many centuries earlier, in Deut. 28:49: "The LORD will bring a nation against you from far away, from the ends of the earth, like an eagle swooping down, a nation whose language you will not understand."

These Chaldeans had no regard for royalty in other nations, for they "mocked" and "scoffed at" them (v. 10a). Such rough treatment of other nations' royalty can be seen in Nebuchadnezzar's treatment of King Jehoiakim and King Jehoiachin, both from Judah. In fact, the Chaldeans went beyond all restraint and exceeded all bounds of decency in the exercise of their cruelty and aggression (v. 11). So proud were they of their cruel conduct that they made a god out of such warfare.

Distress Over the Divine Use of the Wicked

Habakkuk's prayer was certainly answered by the Lord, but in a most astonishing way! The prophet was, of course, deeply perplexed over how the Lord, whose eyes were so pure that he could not look on evil (v. 13), could put up with even the thought of using the Chaldeans as his agents to punish Judah. God indeed was the "Holy One," yet he had "ordained [the Babylonians] to punish" Judah (v. 12). God was Judah's "Rock," and the One who lasted from "everlasting" to eternity. So, this raised some key questions, which Habakkuk put to the Lord: "Why then do you tolerate the treacherous?" "Why are you silent while the wicked swallow up those more righteous than themselves?" (v. 13b–c). Here was a profound theological problem that the prophet could not reconcile with his theology. Judah most assuredly deserved punishment, but how did God ever decide to use a godless executioner to exercise his divine judgment by a people who were decidedly even more wicked than the guilty Judeans?

It seemed as if God was making the Judeans appear like the fish caught in the sea and like the creeping things overtaken on earth, ones that have no ruler over them. Given Babylonian imperialism's astounding record of *inhumanity*, humanity seemed thoroughly exposed to the ruthless whims and wishes of warriors who acted like fishermen rounding up fish, instead of ones coming against human beings. Humans in the hands of these brutes were as defenseless, helpless, and stranded as fish were to the hooks and dragnets of anglers.

The Babylonians worshiped by "sacrific[ing] to their net and burn[ing] incense to their dragnet" (v. 16), for it was from such a haul of these captives that they were enriching themselves without regard to man or God. It was common for militaristic nations to pay divine honors and worship their weapons of war. Once more, however, Habakkuk restated his perplexity in v. 17 after he reminded God how despicable the Babylonians were—as if God were unaware! His question was simply this: Was God going to allow such a destroying nation to go on acting in this manner, especially since they showed no mercy at all? (v. 17b).

Learning to Live by Faith

Since the prophet was unable to reconcile the dilemma he had posed in his prayer-lament to God (1:12–17), he prepared himself to wait to see what God would do, or how he would answer him as he set up a watch on one of the towers of the city wall (2:1). Prophets in the Old Testament were often referred to as "watchmen." From a tower on the city walls, it was possible to view the countryside in all directions and, if necessary, to sound the alarm if danger was coming. So, Habakkuk used the metaphor of a "watchman" as he patiently awaited the Lord's answer to his prayer-lament.

God did answer Habakkuk in a vision, which he was told to write down as a permanent record. By doing so, he was to make it plain on tablets "so that herald may run with it" (2:2). This did not mean the prophet was to make this message so plain, like on a highway billboard, that all could read it without slowing down. No, the Lord meant that all who read it were to run and tell everyone of the impending danger of the Babylonians, for all who were wicked would be under God's judgment, but all who were righteous would be delivered. This divine revelation was to be put into writing because its fulfillment was still future (2:3). So even though its fulfillment seemed to linger, Habakkuk was to keep waiting and watching, for its fulfillment would come to pass (v. 3c).

The Lord began his answer to the prophet by accusing the Babylonians of being proud and greedy. They had an insatiable desire to conquer more lands, and to expand into a larger and larger international empire. They were like drunkards who had no idea when to stop drinking or conquering, for their appetite for conquest and empire was voracious.

However, the righteous person would live by his faith and faith alone (2:4). This was very same promise God made to Abraham in Genesis 15:6. The importance of this theme can hardly be overstated for the history of Israel in that day, or for the Believers in our day. So central was this clause even for Jewish thought that Rabbi Simlai famously remarked: "Moses gave Israel 613 commandments. David reduced them to eleven, Micah to three, Isaiah to two, but Habakkuk to one— 'the righteous shall live by faith.'"

In Hebrew, there are only three Hebrew words for this clause. This text became the heart and soul of much of the Apostle Paul's theology. Yet despite the high reputation of Habakkuk 2:4b, almost every point in this text has been sharply debated over the centuries, even though it was given under the inspiration of the Holy Spirit. All three terms will be examined here.

First, "the righteous" or "the just" is the one who is not "puffed up" or whose soul is not "lifted up" in his own conceits. The contrast between the wicked, who rely on their own might (1:11; 2:4a), and the righteous, who are declared to be such by God, is enormous to say the least. The Hebrew word *sadiq* can also be rendered as "the justified." So, God declares all who believe to be just and free of all legal charges against them.

The phrase "by his faith" (Heb. *'emunah*, 2:4b) is often mistranslated as one's "faithfulness" or "steadfastness," as if the Old Testament saint had to remain an observant Jew by keeping the law of God to be saved. But this more-recent view is incorrect, for what really tips the scales in favor of "by his faith" is that Habakkuk, under the direction of the Spirit of God, deliberately made the connection of this principle with Abraham in Genesis 15:6: Abraham "believed in the LORD; and he counted it to him for righteousness." There is no explicit antecedent for the feminine pronoun "it," so "it" must refer back to "believe" or "belief." Further, in neither the Old nor New Testament was the concept of faith ever separated from its fruits of faithfulness. The distinction between faith and faithfulness is ours, but the division of the grounds and fruit of faith is not a biblical concept.

The third term is "shall live." The life referred to here is our day-to-day living. From the structure of this clause, the phrase "by his faith" modifies "shall live." Therefore, justified persons receive the gift of life by reaching out to God in faith believing.

Verse 5 continued the description of the "puffed up" and "haughty persons" of 2:4a as persons who were deceived by the powers of wine and blinded to the condition of their own actual state of being. Indeed, that is how Babylon fell as an empire on one fateful October night in 539, as most seemed to be dead drunk at Belshazzar's feast. Perhaps while the Babylonians in their drunken stupor boasted of boundless victories and numerous exploits, the city was suddenly taken as the enemy sloshed down the Euphrates and came in under the walls extending over the now-lowered river, which had been drained off its main course into nearby wetlands by Medo-Persian King Cyrus.

What follows in verses 6–20 is divine pronouncement of five woes on the nation of Babylon. The answer to Habakkuk's cry for a public vindication of God's name and righteousness was now at hand. God will now act in condemnation of each of the excesses of Babylon—those things Habakkuk had prayed to God for relief. These items were:

1. *Inordinate greed.* The piles of loot captured from Babylon's enemies had made her wealthy, but it was now payday. The long stretch of extortion of these victim nations was over, and no longer was Babylon going to be able to "put the bite on" these helpless nations. (The words "creditors" and "debtors" come from the Hebrew "to bite," so the pun is accurate!) This was woe number one.

2. *Pride in their formidable walls.* Babylon had deluded itself into thinking her 20-feet-thick, towering walls and even-higher towers were unassailable. She had built most of these fortifications with plunder taken from others, and what she had made she thought was now impregnable. But the stones in the walls would cry out against them to denounce the merciless cruelty of their savage conquests.

3. *Bloodshed atrocities.* The Babylonians built their cities with blood and established them by iniquity. But all the labor of the Chaldeans would be in vain, for all they built would supply the coming fire and their destruction. She was opposed to God, but despite her braggadocio, there was coming a day in which the earth would be filled with the knowledge of the glory of the Lord instead of their

own proud boasts. This event was in the future, but all godless world powers will be overthrown in that final day as the entire world would then come under the rule and reign of Jesus the Messiah (Dan. 2:44; Isa. 2:1–4; Zech. 14:9). Great will be the day of the Lord!

4. *Debauchery to others.* The Babylonians engaged in many forms of debauchery and violence, such as getting their neighbors drunk so they could gaze on their nakedness and skinning them to wallpaper their city walls and places. But God will make this nation drink from his cup of wrath because of the wickedness they had perpetrated on Judah (1:9), Lebanon and neighboring nations (vv. 16c, 17a).

5. *Idolatry.* So what is the value, you Babylonians, to talk to and depend on your lifeless idols? (v. 18). If you think these idols gave you the victory over all those nations in the past, then let them come to your rescue now that destruction is decreed from the One and only true God. Wake up, you dumb stones (v. 19). See if any of you can give any relief or help to your worshipers! But "the LORD is in his holy temple; let all the earth be silent before him" (v. 20). It is time to give reverence and honor to the only true God.

Preface to the Prophet's Prayer to the Lord of History

The prophet prayed in 3:1–2 that God would keep in mind his covenant with Israel when he allowed the Babylonians to come against Judah as chastisement for her sins. Habakkuk had known the work of God in Israel's history, and the fame that God had derived from his interventions in history. For this, he stood in awe and deep respect for God and his work. Therefore, he prayed, *Lord, in our day and in our time, make yourself known to both our foes and to Judah alike, but I beg you, please remember your mercy while you must exercise your wrath* (v. 2d). Habakkuk was inwardly moved, and his body tended to shake in response as he contemplated judgment that must happen because of Judah's wicked disregard of God. He repeated in 3:16 this same consciousness of the awe and terror that must come in the face of the fact that God is holy. But if verses 2 and 16–20 form the framework for this prayer, then verses 3–15 elaborate on that judgment. Nevertheless, he would wait to see what God will do, for God's mercies were new every morning and his faithfulness lasted from generation to generation. His prayer was that God would renew and revive his own work; Habakkuk was not interested in God prospering his own work as a prophet.

God's Theophany in the Past

In this entire passage (3–15), Habakkuk now gives one of the most elaborate and extensive theophanies (descriptions of the appearance of God) in the Old Testament. It is a picture of God's victory and conquest over the whole earth as he establishes his Kingdom to rule and reign over the world forever. It may only be a small taste of what is planned, just as Peter, James and John were given a vision of the resurrected Lord on the Mount of Transfiguration.

The coming of the Lord would be dominant in both parts of this pericope of 3:3–15. Habakkuk looks back at the mighty acts God performed for his people Israel at the exodus and at Mount Sinai. This Hebrew text is archaic in its Hebrew constructions, as it appears to have been deliberately cast into the language reminiscent of the ancient usage, but its meaning is clear. It used the Hebrew word *Eloah* (3:3) as the name for God, a name that occurs 41 times in Job and only 16 times elsewhere in the Old Testament. If "Paran" is to be identified with Sinai (as Deut..33:2 used it), then this prayer-hymn traces the steps as God led Israel in her journey from Egypt to the land of Canaan. We thereby relive the extensive effects of the glory of God as he had acted in the past.

The glory of God depicted here is not the glory reflected in the order of creation, but it is the glory of God that appears because of God's appearances to his people time after time in their history. Each of these points in time was enough to light up the whole creation, for the heavens and the earth were likewise spectators to this same spectacle.

In a comparable manner, the prophet Isaiah saw something similar in the heavenly Temple. The "rays" or "horns" that flashed forth from his hands seemed to point to Moses as he descended from Mount Sinai, being unaware that his face "was radiant" with the glory of God. God is further depicted as the King who is preceded by "plagues" and "pestilence" (v. 5). These events and words were familiar to those who lived through those days, for both "plague" and "pestilence" were also names used for

Canaanite gods named Reshep and Deber. Habakkuk uses these names here to demonstrate God's power over all opposing forces.

The other nations were scared out of their wits by the approach and power of God (v. 6). So real was his presence that the entire world went into convulsions as the Lord of glory came near. Inanimate creation seems to have been much more responsive to the Lord's approach than humans!

The name "Cushan" in v. 7a seems to be a shortened form of Cushan-Rishathaim the first nation to rise to oppress Israel after they came into the land of Canaan. But God used Judge Othniel to deliver Israel on that occasion. The fact that the Lord had provided relief at that time should be a further encouragement for the present and future reliance on him. In the same way, God had provided a reluctant Judge Gideon (Judg. 7:13) to hear the dream of a Midianite as an encouragement to deliver Israel from the ruthless oppression of the Midianites (v. 7b).

God's Theophany for the Future

The text switches from using the third-person pronoun in verses 3–7 to the second-person pronoun in 8–15. Habakkuk began by asking several rhetorical questions (v. 8): "Were you angry with the rivers, Lord?" "Was your wrath [solely] against the streams? "Did you rage against the sea...?" (Josh. 4:23; Ps. 114:3b, 5b). Here were allusions to crossing the Red Sea and the Jordan, which of course would now serve as models for what God could be expected to do in answer to Habakkuk's requests. These were terms borrowed from the old times to depict God's historical interventions when he smote the Red Sea, the Jordan River and the Kishon (Exod. 13:17–14:31; Josh. 3:13–17; 4:21–24). These acts may naturally lead us to expect God to smite the Euphrates in the future (Rev. 16:3–4), for if he is that powerful and that concerned for his people, then he can and will act that dramatically.

In verse 9, our Lord called on the thunder clouds to be part of his personal chariotry and his arsenal of "bow" and "arrows." The mountains cringed before God's mighty power and the enormous torrents of water that poured forth at his command (v. 10). At God's command, the sun failed to appear for an entire day as hailstones from heaven rained down on the fleeing troops as the awesome storm followed the enemy in the same direction (Josh. 10:11–14). This description of God's actions on nature are like those described in Psalm 77:16–20; 50:3; 68:7–8, 32–33.

God's answer to the prophet's question in 3:8 is given in v. 12: No, he was not angry with the rivers or the sea. His anger was against the wickedness of the nations on earth. God would "thrash" (v. 12b) the nations like Gideon thrashed the princes of Zebah and Zalmunna (Judg. 8:16). But God would deliver his people (v. 13), for his "Anointed One" will crush the leader of the land of wickedness as God will triumph over all his enemies in the eschaton (vv. 14–15). The traps the enemy will set up for victims will boomerang and backfire on themselves; the destruction of the godless will be severe and swift.

The Prophet's Confidence for the Future

Habakkuk has been given a picture of the past, present, and future. He began by asking why God does not do something about the unabated evil that goes on in Judah. But when told what God would do in that he would use the Chaldeans to judge Israel, he was perplexed over the fact that God would use a people who obviously were more wicked than Judah as his instrument of judgment. But then God showed Habakkuk how he would vindicate his people and his name in the "day of calamity" (v. 16c). In one of the most amazing pieces of biblical text, Habakkuk asserts that despite the forthcoming tragedies to Judah, "Yet I will rejoice in the LORD, I will joy in the God of my salvation" (v. 18). This was not a resignation to what had to come, nor a case of psychological detachment; it was a demonstration of the fact that with Yeshua as the object of his searching, he could find joy and rejoicing in him. Even though the normal conditions for happiness and joy were absent, such as the fig tree no longer budding, the olive tree no longer producing, the fields being without produce, the cattle pens now no longer occupied with sheep or other cattle (v. 17), it was still possible to rejoice in the Lord. Messiah was more important and more significant than all these things. Habakkuk's testimony was like that of Paul: "Who shall separate us from the love of Messiah? Shall trouble or hardship or persecution or famine or nakedness or danger or sword? … No, in all these things we are more than conquerors through him who loved us" (Rom. 8:35, 37).

Conclusions

1. Here in this slender volume is a grand vision for the working of God on the historical canvas of our day as well as in the past and in the future.
2. Here also is the best definition of what it means to be justified by God and to really live, but to live by faith.
3. But here also is a brief insight into the work that God will do in that future day. The faith of the prophet could and did withstand the test of time, for it did not depend on circumstances that were devoid of suffering: a faith that witnessed one crop failure after another, one that went beyond famine, above health or the access to all the goods for earthly comfort; instead, here was a faith that depended only on a living trust in the Living God.
4. God would remain in charge of history and the nations of the world. His truth would triumph to the blessing of all who put their undivided trust in him.

Questions for Reflection and Discussion

1. Where in the present order of things does God seem to be slow to act against sin, wickedness, or against evil? What is a believer to do in the face of such troubling circumstances?
2. Do you see any problems with God using a more wicked agent to punish people who might seem to be less wicked? Should we quantify evil when trying to make such an assessment of such things?
3. Why does Habakkuk mean when he contrasts the "puffed up" and proud person with the one who is justified by faith? What would be some modern examples of a "puffed up" person?
4. What does "the just shall live by faith" mean? How should we define "the just/righteous" person? What does "shall live" mean? What is the method of coming to the Promised One "by faith"? Is it different from what the New Testament calls being "born again"?
5. Is it possible to rejoice in the midst of trouble and a culture that has gone south? How is this possible? What Scripture would you appeal to vindicate your position?
6. What climactic events at the end of history validate Habakkuk's confidence that history will end well, and that God will be vindicated?

Lesson 9

ZEPHANIAH

"The Great Day of the LORD is Near" – 1:14

Even though Zephaniah is the least-known of the Minor Prophets, he was the one called by God in the seventh century to break the extended period of silence that followed the famous ministry of such famous eighth-century prophets as Isaiah, Hosea, Amos, Micah, and Jonah. Each of the three chapters of Zephaniah is dominated by the two themes of "seek the Lord" and especially "the Day of the LORD," for he presents that day in its worldwide scope, as God discloses his plans for the final events in human history.

Zephaniah's ministry overlapped at least part of the same time that King Josiah reigned in Judah, namely from 640 to 609. His message was the first to be recorded in Scripture for that era, but its scope was wide and complete, for he began with the Lord's universal threat: "'I will sweep everything from the face of the earth,' declares the LORD" (1:2). Thus, the book had an extremely wide sweep in the scope of its message.

The Author Zephaniah

Zephaniah means "the LORD has hidden" or "has caused [me] to be hidden." That name is astounding, since this prophet was born during the years that the wicked King Manasseh reigned (2 Kings 21:16), so it could well be that Zephaniah's name bore witness to the fact that God's power was more than able to preserve those servants of his that trusted in him. This was the period of an enormous amount of innocent bloodshed and brutal violence that filled Jerusalem from one end of the city to the other. Culture and morality had sunk to new lows!

One of the most curious facts connected with this prophet's lineage is that he traces his genealogy back four generations (1:1), when it was normal to give only the name of the prophet's father. This phenomenon has been the subject of much speculation. Some say Zephaniah wanted to make sure he was regarded as a Jew, even though his father's name was "Cushi," which might be rendered as an "Ethiopian" and therefore might classify him as a foreigner. If that were true, then, as Moses taught in Deut. 23:8, a Jew who married a foreigner was not allowed to regard his or her offspring as part of the Jewish community until a pure Jewish pedigree could be established at least three generations later. But more likely is the suggestion that his genealogy extended to the fourth generation to show his connection with the esteemed King Hezekiah, even though only the name "Hezekiah" is given, without "king." But it is still a mystery; if this were so, then why did Zephaniah hesitate to add that he was a "king"? Was he just being humble? It is impossible to know the reason for his action.

No specific date is given for his prophecy except that the word of the Lord came to him "during the reign of Josiah" (1:1), the sixteenth king in Judah, whose reign extended from 640–609. Since Zephaniah's prophecies anticipated the fall of Nineveh in 611–12 (Zeph. 2:13–15), and since 1:4–6 showed the sinful presence of so much pagan idolatry, it seems best to date his book prior to the great revival that came under King Josiah in 621–22, where a number of these evil practices were eliminated (at least partially) as a result of Josiah's revival.

Structure of Zephaniah

Zephaniah exhibits a familiar tripartite division found often in some of the other prophets. But it also has two "hortatory hinges": 2:1–3, which appeal to Judah to "seek the LORD," and 3:8–9, which urges Judah and the nations to "wait for [the LORD]." The resulting outline is something like this:

1. It is Time for the Day of Universal Judgment
2. Hinge #1 – "Seek the LORD" Before the Day of the Lord Comes
3. It is Time to Punish Judah and the Nations
4. Hinge #2 – "Wait for [the Day of the] LORD"
5. It is Time for the Restoration of the Jewish Remnant

We will use this structure as the outline for our discussion of this book.

It's Time for the Day of Universal Judgment

Zephaniah launched right into his message without any "warm-up" comments or introductory statements to get people calm before hearing the news of the threatened judgment. Verses 2–3 see one of the most scorching descriptions of God's wrath that can come against a civilization that has gone ethically and morally mad and has lived in direct opposition to his will. Consequently, everything under heaven must be swept away and removed from the face of the earth, exactly as Paul concluded in Romans 1:18, "For the wrath of God is revealed from heaven against all ungodliness and wickedness of men."

After stating the universal principle of his judgment on all, God narrowed his focus to the mortals he had in mind in vv. 4–6—the men and women of Judah and Jerusalem. The Lord spells out three of Judah's most common sins: idolatry, syncretism, and indifference to the Lord (vv. 4–5). The wicked evidence left from the sinful half-century of Manasseh's long reign, and from the short two-year reign of his son Amon, was more than enough to have corrupted Judah to the maximum (2 Kings 21:1–5; 23:4–14). Judah had served Assyria's idols, worshiped her astral deities, paid adherence to the Canaanite Baals, and given reverence to the Ammonite god Milcom (1 Kings 11:5, 33; 2 Kings 23:13). In fact, Judah had put the statues for worshiping the Canaanite goddess Asherah right inside the temple of the Lord (2 Kings 23:4; 21:7), along with statues of the sun god Shamash (2 Kings 23:11)! So confused and filled with debauchery were the Judahites that they took an oath in the name of God while simultaneously taking an oath in the name of the foreign god Milcom (1:5), just as in our day we have confused believers saying: "Christians and Muslims worship the same god," or some contemporary believers equate Jesus with Buddha, Sun Myung Moon or whatever other cult leader there is today. But the Lord taught in Exodus 20:3, "You shall have no other gods before [besides] me." Furthermore, Yeshua taught in Matthew 6:24, "No one can serve two masters. Either he will hate the one and love the other, or he will be devoted to the one and despise the other. You cannot serve both." Judah was now in full retreat from the God she had pledged to love and serve. No longer did they "seek the LORD nor inquire of him" (Zeph. 1:6).

The people of Judah were told, "Hush! Be silent! For "the Day of the LORD is near" (v. 7). The reason for such silence is this: The Lord has prepared a feast, and guess who has been invited? The Babylonians! They will be God's instruments for carrying out his judgment against Judah (v. 10). The figure of God inviting the wicked to such a feast is found elsewhere in the prophets as well.

Judah had also adopted the customs and habits of the nations around them, for their princes, officials and the king's sons were all "clothed in foreign apparel" (v. 8). They also avoided stepping on the threshold of their temple as the priests of Dagon practiced in the Philistine pagan temple of their idol, after Dagon literally fell apart on the threshold floor of their temple in the presence of the Ark of the Covenant.

The announcement of the "Day of the LORD" is the most prominent feature in the book of Zephaniah (1:14, 15), as it was in the book of Joel (2:1; 3:14). The battle cry of the Lord would go up against Judah on that day. It would begin at the "Fish Gate" (1:10b), where the fishermen from the coastal city of Tyre usually brought their catch to sell (see Nah 13:16), and also that cry would go up in the "New/Second Quarter," (2 Kings 22:14), where Manasseh had added a wall near the Fish Gate to include a new suburb in the city of Jerusalem. The cry would go up in "Mortar," the pounding place or valley basin that was between the east and west hills of Jerusalem (what is known as the Tyropaean Valley), where the merchants and traders resided—Jerusalem's "Wall Street." Zephaniah declared that that day would be:

A day of wrath,
A day of distress and anguish,
A day of trouble and ruin,
A day of darkness and gloom,
A day of clouds and blackness (1:15).

God's anger and wrath were not capricious, nor were they vindictive acts aimed at the innocent as well; it was God's holy character aimed at sin. Nothing of this world's goods, such as silver or gold, shall in that day be given in exchange for being excused from God's justified anger. That day would not be limited to just a single day for it embraced every instance of divine judgment that had fallen upon the nation of Israel in the past but was also a token or sample of the combination of acts God would let loose on that final time of his anger on the "Day of the LORD." In the anxiety and distress of that time, mortals shall wander about as if they were blind, not knowing what to do (1:17). The prophet Ezekiel also foretold how the wicked in that time of God's judgment would toss their silver in the streets and treat their gold as if it were junk and unclean.

Often the body of Believers have used Zephaniah 1:14–18 in its eschatology, as seen in 1 Thessalonians 5:1–10; 4:13–18; 2 Thessalonians 1:5–7; Matthew 25:14–15, 19–29; 25–1–13, thereby also equating the "Day of the LORD" with the *Parousia*, i.e., the second coming of our Lord, and with the resurrection of the dead, and the Last Judgment.

"Seek the LORD" Before the Day of the LORD Comes

Since such an awful judgment is coming, Zephaniah urged all mortals to repent before this all takes effect; they must "seek the LORD," as Amos 5:6 and Isaiah 55:6 urged. All those who will humble themselves before the Lord and seek him will be hidden on the day of his anger (2:3). Zephaniah pauses amid his horrific announcements to urge his people not to be careless but to seek the Lord and to be humble before him. They, and we today, must exhibit a meekness of spirit (Isa. 11:4) and a contriteness of heart (Ps. 34:18). We must turn to God in obedience, for without it, how can we express the reality of the faith that results in righteousness?

It's Time to Punish Judah and the Nations

The judgment of God will not only strike Judah in that day (1:4–7), but it will also come over the Philistine cities. Four are mentioned here: Gaza, Ashkelon, Ashdod and Ekron (2:4–7), as well as the countries of Moab and Ammon, Cush, and Assyria (2:8–15). It was believed that the Philistines had come from Caphtor, and known as "Cherethites," which the Septuagint rendered as "Crete" (see Amos 9:7). The coastlands of the former territory occupied by the Philistines, but today known as the Gaza Strip, will be so devoid of its inhabitants on that day so that those coastlands will serve as pastures for the nomadic shepherds and their flocks (v. 7). That land, God promises, will belong to his people Israel, after he brings them back from captivity in Babylon so that in the end day the people of Israel and Judah will return from the four corners of the earth.

The theology of the return of the remnant does not have its beginnings in Zephaniah but is found at least as far back in the prophets as the ninth century B.C.E., for both Obadiah and Joel had predicted Israel would once again "possess their possessions." Amos stated the same promise in the eighth century—that Israel would emerge from her sifting among the nations to be restored back in the land of Israel (5:15; 9:11). This hope of being restored to the land is also found in Micah 4:6–7, Daniel 7:21–27 and more.

Next God turns to the two nations that were descendants of Lot—Moab and Ammon (2:8–11). Instead of their realizing their own salvation was offered through the blessing that God would communicate to them through Israel (Gen. 12:3), they insisted on reviling Israel with constant reproaches and continually violating Israel's borders. It was their pride and arrogance (2:10) that was their downfall, added the Lord (Isa. 16:6; Jer. 48:29; Ezek. 25:1–7). Thus, these two nations earned punishment by heaping curses on Israel, which Genesis 12:3 had warned against any nation doing if it wished to be blessed. God announced that these two nations would end up as Sodom and Gomorrah did, two cities once geographically near these two nations until they were destroyed with fire and brimstones from heaven. One day soon God will destroy all the false gods on earth (2:11), for then men and women, including Gentiles and Jews, from all over the earth will come to bow down before the Lord as the only true God. This event is also described in Isaiah 2;2, Micah 4:1–2 and Zechariah 8:22; 14:16.

God also judged Ethiopia, the first time when he sent the Babylonians against Cush and its ally Egypt (2:12; 2 Kings 24:7; Ezek. 30:4–9). Later, even the Persians, Greeks and Romans took over the land of Ethiopia. In like manner, God will also "stretch his hand against the north and destroy Assyria and make Nineveh desolate" (2:13), as Zephaniah's contemporary, Nahum, had likewise declared. Instead of a robust and teeming population, Nineveh would now be a resting place for wild birds and beasts (2:14). Nineveh may have lived it up high in her day, thinking she was impregnable because of the size, strength, and the extent of her fortifications, but she was slated to end up as a ruin (2:15). Her conquests under Sennacherib and Ashurbanipal had made her giddy with pride and confidence as she brutally robbed the nations around her, but those days would soon be history.

Zephaniah returns once more to Jerusalem and Judah in 3:1–7. That city was guilty of accepting no correction; she did not trust the Lord himself and refused to draw near to God (3:2). Jerusalem was characterized more by oppression, rebellion, and faithlessness (3:1). She was a mess in every way one could think ethically, morally, or religiously about a city or a nation. Her officials were as greedy as the Gentile nations that were coming against her; they were "evening wolves who left nothing for the morning" (3:3)! Her prophets were just as bad, for they were unprincipled and as treacherous as the general population (3:4a). In like manner, her priests violated the law of God and profaned his sanctuary (3:4b). Goodness and kindness were nowhere to be found in Judah.

In contrast to such raw disregard for the things of God, the Lord was altogether righteous and every day he gave evidence of his justice (3:5). But the Lord had to judge Judah as well as the nations, wanting thereby to call both to repentance, but no one heeded the call or paid attention to his righteous and just acts (3:5–7). Had not God given Israel, under King David's rule, authority to subjugate all the nations round about her so Israel was undisturbed by the threat of invasion? But that had long been forgotten. Instead, Israel had thought that based on the promise-plan of God, she was exempt from all these attacks and immune from any destruction, regardless how they lived! God, they incorrectly thought, would save them from all of that. How wrong they were!

"Wait for the [Day of] the LORD"

Because Judah had acted so poorly, they were told, "Wait for me;" that is, wait for the Day of the LORD. Here again was the central theme of this book. For that day would soon appear when the Lord would gather all the nations and then pour out his wrath on them (3:8b–d). The Lord had previously given this announcement in the book of Joel (3:1–2), and he would announce it later again in Zechariah (14:1–3). Matthew 25:31–33 repeated the same warning. The whole world would be subject to the "fire of [his] jealousy" (3:8e). There was one hot time coming for all the wicked.

It's Time for the Restoration of the Jewish Remnant

However, after the time of God's judgment had been completed, God himself would gather and assemble the remnant of his people Israel and the remnant of the nations of the world, so all could return to their land to worship him with a new purity and holiness as was rarely observed throughout history. He would purify the lips of Israel and the Gentiles alike so they together could call on the name of the Lord (3:9). Both Jews and Gentiles had taken on their lips the names of heathen gods, who were no gods at all, and thus had polluted those lips; thus, they needed to be purified (see Ps. 16:2; Hos. 2:17). At the second advent of our Lord, God would destroy all those who were antagonistic to him. But when he purified the lips of all believers, then Jews and Gentiles would be able to speak the same language of faith and serve him with one accord. In fact, the very same virtues Zephaniah listed here resulted from a purified remnant were like those that Yeshua taught about in the Sermon on the Mount. He taught:

1. Blessed are the meek, for they will inherit the earth.

2. Blessed are those who hunger and thirst for righteousness.

3. Blessed are the peacemakers. (Matt. 5:5–6, 8–9)

The prophet then urged the people: "Sing, daughter Zion, shout aloud Israel! Be glad and rejoice with all your heart, Daughter Jerusalem" (3:14), and then he gave a list of reasons for such jubilation:

1. "The LORD has taken away your punishment" (v. 15a). That punishment had been for their sins, but now that her sin had been removed, they were free of the judgment, and it was time to rejoice for their new status in Messiah.

2. "The LORD has turned back your enemy" (v. 15b). God would not only overthrow the Babylonians, but he would intervene on behalf of Israel in the final day to rid them of all their enemies, finally (3:19a).

3. "The LORD, the King of Israel, is with you, never again will you fear any harm" (v. 15c). If there would be no more fear of anyone harming them, then this promise of God must be fulfilled at the end of history when Israel had been restored to the land and the Lord had returned a second time to earth.

4. "The LORD your God is with you, the Mighty Warrior who saves you. He will take great delight in you; in his love he will no longer rebuke you but will rejoice over you with singing" (v. 17a). This was not completely fulfilled when Yeshua came to earth the first time, so it must be reserved for his second advent. In his first advent, John said: "He came unto his own, and his own received him not" (John 1:11), But now in his second advent he will be silent, for there is now nothing to denounce or any reason to rebuke them (3:8).

5. "I will remove from you all who mourn over the loss of your appointed festivals, which is a burden and a reproach for you" (v. 18a). All during their exile, the Israelites had been unable to worship the Lord with proper offerings, feasts or to celebrate his holy days, but now there will be appropriate provisions made to remedy that situation, even if modifications were needed (Ezek. 40:1–46:24). The exile and the loss of the land of Canaan had brought reproach on Israel, but that burden and reproach would also be lifted in that day.

To conclude his message, Zephaniah pulls together several things God will do for Israel:

1. "I will deal with all who have oppressed you" (v. 19a). Not only would the Lord restore his people to their land once again, but he would accompany that work with his destruction of all who had afflicted or oppressed Israel. This he would do based on Genesis 12:3—by cursing all who had cursed Israel. Israel has always been God's first love, whom he regarded as his bride, and he declared himself to be her husband (Jer. 3:14). Of course, God had had to chastise her at times, even harshly, but he had never thought of casting her off totally; she would be his wife forever (Hos. 2:14–20). She would be known as "the apple of his eye" (Deut. 32:10; Zech. 2:8). God had warned that those who touched Israel would be regarded as his enemy (Jer. 2:3; Zeph. 2:8–11; Ezek. 25:1–7). Even though God may have used hostile nations to judge Israel, these nations were to remember that they were still in the hand of God (Isa 10:12–13). Otherwise, all mortals are to bless Israel and pray for the peace of Jerusalem (Ps. 122:6).

2. "I will rescue the lame" (v. 19b). God knows the needs of the nation of Israel down to their exact details.

3. "I will gather the exiles" (v. 19c). They will not be forgotten no matter where they have migrated to.

4. "I will give them praise and honor in every land where they have suffered shame" (v. 19d–e).

5. "I will gather you; at that time, I will bring you home" (v. 20a). This promise must not be dropped out of Scripture, for there are over 140 expressions of this same promise of God regathering his people Israel back to their land throughout Scripture.

6. "I will give you honor and praise among all the people of the earth, when I restore your fortunes before your very eyes" (v. 20c–d).

What fantastic promises! What a magnificent Lord!

Conclusions

1. The "Day of the LORD" will conclude history and be awesome in its effects on the earth.

2. In the meantime, Israel and the nations of the world are to "seek the LORD."

3. There will be a believing remnant in Israel and among the Gentiles that will be rescued by the Lord.

4. Such a rescue will be reason enough for hilarious and universal rejoicing and praise to God.

5. Finally, all oppressors of Israel will be silenced and will trouble her no longer by the decree of God.

6. God will give the land of Canaan to Israel as part of his eternal promise.

Questions for Reflection and Discussion

1. Is the judgment of God described in this book too much and "over the top" for your view of the kindness and gentleness of our God? How would you explain such statements to someone who is reading the Bible for the first time considering the parallel strong emphasis in the Bible on the love of God?

2. How certain is the promise that God will maintain his promise of a Seed, his promise of the land and his promise of the Gospel until he returns to the earth a second time? What are some of the key passages? How many such promises are there in the prophets? Why is this promise so often spiritualized in the Church? Is replacement theology taught in Scripture? If so, where?

3. What pagan nations are affected by Zephaniah's prophecy? How will that affect Israel's land in the final day?

4. How will the threat of a universal judgment over the entire world affect the United States of America? How is that tied into the Abrahamic Covenant of Genesis 12:2–3?

Lesson 10

HAGGAI

"From This Day on, I Will Bless You" – 2:19c

The book of Haggai may be small, but over the years it has had an enormous impact at various times and on different cultures. For example, just two years after Columbus sailed for America, Savonarola, often called the "morning star of the Reformation," preached a series of messages on the book of Haggai, in which he gave an urgent call for repentance on the part of the civil and religious leaders of that day. After four years of preaching, Savonarola's voice was silenced as he was hung publicly in disgrace as a heretic and his body was burned, and his ashes thrown into the Arno River.

No less significant was the preaching of John Knox (1514–1572) on the Haggai that led the nation of Scotland to a memorable time of reformation and renewal before God. So, we should not judge a book either by its cover or by its size. This book has had an enormous impact over the years!

The Author of Haggai

Haggai's writing ministry lasted a mere five months in the year 520. We know little of his background. He is identified repeatedly as "the prophet" (1:1, 3; 2:1, 10) and as "the LORD's messenger/angel" (1:13), His name means "festival," which suggests he may have been born on one of Israel's feast days. Haggai's father's name is not given, as was customary in some of the other prophet's books, nor is his father mentioned in Ezra 5:1 or 6:14. He was a contemporary of Zechariah; both men were used by God to prod the recently returned exiles from Babylon to pick up the building of the temple that had laid dormant from 536–520 due to a squabble that broke out among the returnees. The task of these two prophets was to help the returned exiles overcome their disillusionment, discouragement, disheartened spirits, and the controversy over the modest size of the footprints for the building on the second temple dedicated to the Lord. Both these men called God's people to deal with their indifference and disputes and confess to him their complacency, apathy, and faulty priorities.

Historical Background to Haggai

The 38 prose verses in this book are unusual, for most of the prophets preferred to use a form of poetic address to the people. Haggai refers to himself in the third person, but it is possible that one of his disciples or a secretary collected and arranged his messages in written form.

It is important to realize where we are in history at the time Haggai was ministering. Sixty-six years earlier, Jerusalem had been decimated by King Nebuchadnezzar of Babylon. This included the destruction of the temple Solomon had dedicated to the Lord in 967. Thus, the people of Israel did not have a place to worship for the first time since Moses built the tabernacle, the forerunner of Solomon's temple. The temple lay in ruins at that time as most of Israel's population had been forced into exile some 500+ miles away, in what is today Iraq. Nebuchadnezzar left a small cadre of Jews in Israel, but since they were devoid of a place of worship and without solid leadership, their resolve melted as most of them disobediently fled to Egypt and abandoned the land God had promised to give to them. It was a period of deep spiritual stagnation and total rebellion against God.

Then in 539, the international picture changed abruptly as a new power in the Near East emerged: the combined nations of Media-Persia, under Cyrus' masterful leadership. Babylon itself had met her promised demise on the very same night she sponsored a feast that was described and witnessed by Daniel (Dan. 5). There was a lightning blitzkrieg invasion by Cyrus, and the city was overrun by his army. Babylon was taken without an arrow fired or a spear thrust. King Belshazzar had previously retreated to the capital city of Babylon, thinking he had more than 20 years of supplies to last in case of an extended siege of the city, but Cyrus outsmarted him by diverting the waters of the Euphrates that flowed under the walls, and through Babylon, thus letting him march into that fortified city by sloshing down the now-lowered riverbed as he and his army ducked under the walls of the city. All this was taking place as the banqueters were toasting their pagan idol-god Marduk with the vessels stolen from God's temple.

As early as 538, Cyrus issued a decree (recorded in Ezra 1:2–4; 6:2–5) that made it possible for those exiled from their native lands to return and even build a house/temple for their God. Under Governor Zerubbabel and High Priest Joshua, almost 50,000 Jews decided to return to the land of Israel, but this was a disappointingly small number, for most Jewish people had settled down to a comfortable life in Babylon.

At first, the returnees to Jerusalem were united "as one person" (Ezra 3:1) in their resolve to rebuild the fallen temple of the Lord. They began by building an altar to God for their sacrifices (Ezra 3:2, 3–6). But even more significantly, in the second month of the second year of their return (Ezra 3:8), they began work on the second temple. Soon the footers for the foundation of the temple were laid, but trouble broke out between the older exiles who remembered the beauty, splendor, and greater size of the Solomonic Temple and the younger generation that rejoiced to see the temple underway. What they were now building was, to the oldsters, a scaled-down model of the former building. The younger generation, who had not seen the original temple by Solomon, were delighted the project was now underway, but confusion and discord arose between the gripes of the older people and the shouts of joy from the younger people, and one could not tell which was more prominent. Amid all this confusion came an offer from the polyglot people of Samaria to help build the temple, but Zerubbabel refused, because the Samaritans were by this time a mixture of Gentiles and Jews. The Assyrians had deliberately intermingled Gentile foreigners with some of the leftovers from the northern tribes of Israel (Ezra 4:3). The governor said, "You have no part with us in building a temple to our God" (Ezra 4:3). That led to more trouble, for the Samaritans were now so incensed over being refused a part in this project that they wrote to the Medo-Persian administration to get an injunction to halt the work. With this work-stoppage order, the building project came to a halt, and there matters stood until the second year of King Darius, when God also stirred up the spirits of Haggai and Zechariah with a message that called for the restarting of the work in 520. A chronology of these days would include:

539 – The fall of Babylon

538 – Cyrus's decree to allow a return home

537 – 49,897 Jews return home (Neh. 7; Ezra 2)

536 – Work on the Temple stopped (Ezra 3)

530 – King Cyrus dies

530–522 – Cambyses II, Cyrus's son reigns

522–486 – Darius I (civil war; Behistun Stone erected)

520 – Darius I confirms Cyrus's Decree about the temple (Ezra6)

520 – Haggai's and Zechariah's messages to rebuild temple

516 – Second Temple finally completed (Ezra 6:15)

It is Time to Renew the Work of God

These two chapters of Haggai are seldom referred to for a sermon in our day, unless a particular church announces a new building plan is about to get underway, but it is important to note that this book serves well also as a metaphor for the broader principle that all impediments to renewing the work of God must be resisted, and the Lord and his work must take priority of our lives as believers. This is why Haggai began by urging us to refuse our penchant for using any excuses that would preempt the work of God. It is also significant that the dateline for this prophecy was no longer based on the dates of the Davidic kings, as had been customary up to this point; it was now the "second year of King Darius," for the "times of the Gentiles" had arrived. Haggai's message, then, became the first word from the Lord in this post-exilic era and new times of the Gentiles, even though Ezekiel and Daniel had delivered God's word during the 70 years of exile.

Stop Making Excuses

Haggai's first message came in the sixth month and the first day of that month. Since this was a holiday, in this day off work as a day of rest, it would be a time to recall all God had done for his people and everyone. But it also signaled in an ominous way the harvest time, for the grape, fig and pomegranate harvests would also signal that the end of the summer fruits had also come. There may be a trace of Jeremiah's mournful note here, when he said in Jeremiah 8:20, "The summer is over and we are not yet saved." Amos signaled a similar note in Amos 8:1 where he had a vision of a basket of summer fruit; that commodity in Hebrew sounds very much like the Hebrew word for the "end" that may have come upon Israel. So there may have been more than just its location in time; it may also have carried overtones and some of the signs of the times they were living in!

God's word was addressed first to the nation's two leaders: Zerubbabel the governor and Joshua the High Priest. Zerubbabel was the grandson of Jehoiachin; thus, he was in the Davidic Messianic line. Zerubbabel means "seed of Babylon" or "shoot of Babylon." He was called a "governor," a word borrowed from the Babylonian Akkadian language, and he probably was the same person who is called Sheshbazzar in Ezra 1:8 and 5:14, for the work Sheshbazzar does in Ezra 5:18 is attributed to Zerubbabel in Ezra 3:8.

Zerubbabel's name brings up a story of God's supernatural providence, for that story begins with King Coniah (also called Jehoiachin) in Jeremiah 22:30. There God declared Jehoiachin "childless," which meant no child of his would sit on the throne of David in Judah from his line. Thus the "signet seal" was stripped from him, as he and his five sons landed in captivity and were made eunuchs, as Isaiah 39:7 described. As a result of this action, Jehoiachin adopted the seven sons of Neri, who also was a descendant of David, but who came from David's son Nathan rather than from Solomon's line. Amazingly, then, the line of David, which originally had come through Solomon, terminated with Jehoiachin, but continued to be connected to David's house and line through Neri's son Shealtiel. But Shealtiel also died childless, so his brother Pediah had to perform the duty of Levirate (brother-in-law) marriage (Deut. 25:5–10), out of which Zerubbabel was born, who then was the legal son of Shealtiel but the actual son of Pediah, another descendant of David from David's son Nathan. Wow! What a complicated line! But it held true to what God had predicted! Joshua was the High Priest and a descendant in the line of High Priests from Zadok.

Let us go back to the excuses that the people now raised to working on the Second Temple. God noticed that "this people say, 'the time has not come, the time that the LORD's house should be built" (Hag. 1:2). Here was another rarity, for seldom, even in the times of the Lord's frequent berating of Israel did he previously distance himself from his people by noting "*this* people say." They always had been "*my* people." But it was evident that God was extremely displeased with them. This was caused by their excuse-making. In fact, when the people said "the time" has not come to build the house of the Lord, they were merely using a circumlocution for saying it was God's fault the temple had not yet been built. Their thinking must have been something like this: *If God wants his house to be built, then times need to change so we can recoup the huge losses we have sustained from our defeat as a nation and our exile in Babylon. The economy must improve, the shekel must increase in its value and political relations with our neighbors must improve.* The exiles were blaming God for their inefficiency and procrastination by saying "the time" instead of defiantly and directly pointing to God. However, they must have pointed their fingers toward heaven when they gave their explanation for sixteen years of the work-stoppage on the temple! We mortals are quick to drag up excuses that shift the blame from ourselves to God or others, but these excuses are mere pretext for our own laziness and selfish reinvestment of our time. However, the returnees amazingly did have time to somehow build their own homes.

Make First Things First

Haggai urged God's people to make his work come before their own, for the task given to us by the King of kings was top priority. The prophet pointedly asked in v. 4, "Is it time for you yourselves to dwell in your paneled homes [while] this temple lie[s] in ruins?" It was clear that the religious condition of the people's hearts could be gauged by their attitude toward working on the house of God. This was a sort of spiritual barometer; in fact, to neglect God's house would amount to a patent violation of their claim that God was their Lord and King. It amounted to outright treason; there was no other way to put it. They had made him "Lord," but without any real authority or evidence that he was indeed Lord over their lives.

But rejecting God's call to work on his house was like inviting him to reject their labors on their own projects. The people pretended to be too poor to finance the work, yet all the while they were lavishly spending and upgrading their own homes. How could that have happened? This made their excuses nothing but a lie. The prophet cried out, "Consider your ways" (1:5). Haggai used that phrase four times (1:5, 7; 2:15, 18). He gave an urgent call for his compatriots to search their own hearts and live in this unbalanced situation. This was idolatry, for anytime we put any person, goal, idea, etc. ahead of the Living God, it is idolatry.

The only solution is to put God's ways ahead of our own plans, goals, or aspirations. Haggai used a series of Hebrew infinitive absolutes (which put the stress on the actions themselves) from the Lord to question the people. Were they sowing more and yet harvesting less in recent days? Were they eating and drinking more and yet feeling less well-fed and full? Were they wearing more clothes and yet feeling less warmth? Were they earning more money and yet finding they had not enough to buy what they used to? There was the point: No one cheats God without also cheating themselves.

One cannot help seeing that our Lord wanted us to see the correlation between the productivity of the land and our spiritual growth. Ever since man's fall in Eden, this principle has remained in force. This is the point Amos made in 4:6–10. Five times God sent one calamity after another to a people tone-deaf to his call to repent. The calamities were given to get people's attention. But none of these calamities had any effect. Five times in these verses in Amos the description of the calamity ended, "Yet you did not return to the LORD." Consequently, the prophet ended up declaring to the people of Amos' day, "Prepare to meet your God!" That was not a salvation text; it was a judgment text in which God counted to five and then said they were "out"—next came God's judgment.

We Must Get Involved in the Work of the Lord

Once more in v. 7, Haggai begged his audience to ponder carefully what was going on here. God instructed the people through his servant Haggai to go to the mountains and cut down timber and begin to build (v. 8). But this instruction raised another question: Didn't the people receive from Cyrus permission to get cedar logs and masonry from the forests of Lebanon and from the hills nearby when they first returned? What had happened to that supply of materials that had accumulated 16 years ago? Is that how the people had built their fancy paneled homes—from stolen materials left from the abandoned Temple? The text makes no accusations, but what had been provided was no longer available; someone had taken it! So where had it all gone?

The purpose in building the temple was not realized in seeing the building itself; instead, the building was first and last meant to bring pleasure to God and to glorify him (v. 8). God's pleasure comes not merely from buildings being raised, but from the attitudes and conditions of the hearts of his people who did the work and contributed to this building.

What if we fail to obey God's call to get involved in his work? What will we lose if we chose to go the route of pleasing ourselves instead of God? Verse 9 answers that: When we look for much, it will come to little. What little we brought home; God would blow on and it would disappear. But why would God do that to you or me, or to Israel? It was, as Haggai described, because his house lay in ruins, and everyone was invested in their own projects (v. 9b). This text repeated the theology of Deuteronomy 28:22–24. The cost of disobeying God is expensive. It is never a shortcut to success. Because God's house was in "ruins" (Heb. *hareb*), God had called for a "drought" (*horeb*) on the land, the mountains, the grain, new wine, and olive oil (v. 11). God loved his people so much that when they refused to hear his words of rebuke, he would try to get their attention once again by calling for a drought on their crops and on the work of their hands.

The Beauty of Obedience

Here is a rare verse in the Bible, for starting with the leaders of the people and continuing down through the ordinary people, with one accord all the men and women "obeyed the voice of the LORD their God" (v. 12). The preaching of Haggai, and the convicting power of the Holy Spirit, brought beautiful results to the praise of God.

In only 24 days since he gave his message, now the people began the work on God's house. God's word of assurance was theirs, for he promised: "I am with you, says the LORD" (v. 13). That was no empty mantra, but a reality that would be realized as the people put their shoulders to the work. Moreover, God "stirred up" (v. 14) the leaders and the people as their vision and energy was renewed and a complete change of heart was in evidence.

Do Not Demean What Appears to Be Small Doings in the Work of God

It is always easy, if one has a mind to do so, to make invidious comparisons between different parts or times in the work of God. The first Temple of Solomon was no doubt spectacular indeed, but to compare it with what was going up currently under the hands of an obedient people was to incite despondency and despair. First, no humanly constructed building is going to be equal to the glory and magnificence of God himself. A house built by mortals will never rival the splendor of heaven or of God (1 Kings 8:27); that was true even of Solomon's Temple. Israel had to face this problem head-on: Did this new Temple seem, at least in their eyes, like nothing at all? (2:3). But mark it down, it was on the twenty-first day of the seventh month, on the last day of the Feast of Tabernacles, the builders heard a novel word from God as they took off a whole week to celebrate the Feast of Tabernacles and for Yom Kippur (Day of Atonement). The work on the Temple had only gone on for 21 days, so little progress could be detected, especially as the materials had to be regathered and resorted.

But God's word to those who may have been disappointed by such meager results in the first 21 days was to repeat three times over, "be strong" (2:4), the same command he had to give to Joshua and to David. The people of Israel were to be strong, and to rally round to do the work, for God was also at work among them. If they felt weak, his strength would come to peak performance (2 Cor. 12:9; Heb. 13:21). Zechariah sounded this same note when he urged, "Let your hands be strong" (8:9).

God had given his promise long ago when he brought Israel out of Egypt, so he was still on track carrying out his plan (2:5; Gal. 3:8). Was this not the same promise he had made when he led the exodus? (Exod. 29:45). In addition to his strength and presence with them, God promised his Spirit would be among the builders (2:5b). Regrettably, we contemporaries do not emphasize the ministry of the Holy Spirit in times of the Old Testament, but without the work of the Spirit then, where would God's regenerating grace, or for that matter any other work of God, come from, and where would the enablement of God's men and women originate? (John 3:10; Psalm 51:11).

The future belonged to the Lord, for he would establish his Kingdom on earth. Our Lord had already shaken the earth once, even if only slightly—at the Exodus from Egypt (Ps. 114) and at Sinai (Exod. 19:18; Hab. 3:6), but very soon he would shake this old planet like nothing it had ever felt (2:6; 2 Pet. 3:10–11). This ought to convince us to hold on to those things that cannot be shaken. I experienced a taste of what that might be like on September. 13, 1988 when I was teaching in Kingston, Jamaica. Hurricane Gilbert blew onto that island at 200 miles per hour. That shook everything apart on that island. But God has a Kingdom that will never be shaken. In that coming day, God will shake all the nations of this world and then shall come to the "Desire" of all nations.

Translators miss the fact that here is a reference to the Messiah, so they badly translate this word to "desired things," "precious things," "treasure," or "wealth" of all the nations. However, King Saul was called "the desire of Israel" (1 Sam. 9:20), and Daniel 9:23; 10:11, 19 refers to the Antichrist, who does not have the "desire of women"—all using the plural forms and the same Hebrew consonants as are found in Haggai 2:7. Therefore, we are still of the conviction that "Desire" refers to the Messiah who will come.

God promised, in addition to giving us an unshakeable kingdom and a Messianic King, that he would fill this Temple under construction with his glory (2:7). It all belonged to the Lord: the silver, the gold (2:8–9), the land on which it sat, and all who worshiped in it.

A Call for Personal Holiness

Haggai had addressed the nation's unwarranted *contentment* in his first message and their unwarranted *discontent* in his second message, but now in his third message he addressed their *misplaced values*. This third message came on the "twenty-fourth day of the ninth month," exactly three months after the people had responded to Haggai's initial call to get to work on the Temple. Once again Haggai began by calling them to "think, think, think," i.e., to carefully consider (2:15) the question: Is holiness catchy? (2:11–12). Can it be communicated to the third degree? The people must have reasoned that now the Temple was underway, all would be well, and everyone could relax in their efforts to serve the Lord, with the Temple as a talisman. The question arises about whether the

Bible taught indirect communication of holiness to the third degree. Haggai taught that holy acts have no power to make persons holy; only God can. The Temple is indeed holy, but it does not automatically sanctify the land of Judah and its people, even if they worked to build it. So it also is true that just because we had grandparents who knew and walked with God, that things would go all right for us too. Building the Temple would not serve as a good-luck charm to ward off evil or the calamities permitted by God.

If trusting in a good-luck charm was the ditch they could fall into on one side of the road, the ditch on the other side was the misconception that worshiping in the Temple would automatically cleanse unholy persons.

A second question was posed for the priests: Is evil and defilement contagious? (v. 13). Yes, it could easily be transmitted from one person to another, just as one rotten apple in a bushel basket would affect all the apples it touched. The point then was this: Holy works do not make holy persons (v. 14). If the people were trusting in their work of rebuilding the Temple as an automatic "open-sesame" for the whole country and for all past failures, their logic was flawed. Only cleansed men and women can serve God with clean hands and a clean heart. Righteousness does not come from what a person does for God but from what a person is in their hearts before him. Depending on environmental determinism to correct or protect us and other children, as some all too readily do in sending their children to Sunday School, was just as faulty if that is all we had to lean on!

The curses found in v. 17 were the same ones Deuteronomy 28:22 had warned would come if there was no revival and repentance among the people. Haggai asked, "Was the seed [for sowing] still in the barn?" (v. 19). Of course, it had better not have been in the barn, because the ground with this seed needed to catch the rainy season to grow. But watch from now on, for since you have turned in your hearts and begun to rebuild the Temple, the land will go from producing bad harvests to good ones. God's favor could indeed be reflected even in the production of the crops!

In the same way, notice how the health and productivity of the grape vines, fig trees, olive trees and pomegranates have shown such good increase since the day you wholeheartedly turned back to God in repentance (v. 19). Progress in the spiritual realm became one of the first indications of progress in the agricultural realm as well.

For a second time, God spoke to Zerubbabel through Haggai (2:20–21) in words like 2:6–9. God would send a shake-up in that eschatological day in the future, in connection with the second advent of our Lord. Haggai explained what that day would be like by going back in history for an analogy to explain his point. As God overthrew Sodom and Gomorrah, so the kingdoms of the world would collapse under his power in that last day. To use another analogy, as Gideon overwhelmed the Midianites and they turned their swords on each other in self-destruction in the darkened confusion (Judg. 7:22), so it will happen on that final day. As Pharaoh and his army "went down" from their horses and chariots into the sea and were lost, so God will vanquish horse and rider in the final day. History was full of analogies of what God would do in the future. The past would give us a brief insight into the future work of God!

In the prophet's final prediction, God would take the Davidic scion of Governor Zerubbabel and make him a "signet ring," for he had been chosen by God (2:23). Zerubbabel is called God's "Servant," which is the most frequently used title for the coming Messiah. The God-ordained emblem of the office, and authority of the Davidic descendant, was the "Signet Ring," which had been taken from one of David's seed, Jehoiachin (Jer. 22:24) and given to another in the line of David. Yeshua, of course, came to earth as a man in the race and family of David, for he always was and would remain God as well. Great would be the Day of the Lord!

Conclusions

1. God will not accept our lame excuses for our lack of involvement in his work. They will be shown for what they were!

2. We must get our priorities straight and put God's work and his honor and glory first and ahead of our own work and projects.

3. Holiness is not contagious; it comes from a holy God to hearts and lives that have been responsive to our Lord and his word.

4. Evil and wickedness, however, is contagious and is easily picked up in the absence of a vital life lived with the Lord.

5. One day God will rock this old globe as he appears for the second time on earth to rule and reign forever.

6. At the heart of the second return is the coming of Yeshua, the Davidic Messiah.

Questions for Reflection and Discussion

1. How do we avoid being pressured by the majority, or by the tyranny of the urgent that needs to be tended to, when we are called upon by God to set new priorities for his honor and glory?

2. When we become resistant to the message of the Word of God, does he in his love try to get our attention by speaking to us through our national debt, the gross national product rate, the value of our money, and the crop production rates? Is this just an Old Testament situation, or is it still operative in our day as well?

3. Is holiness just as catchy as evil? Can we trust environmental influences to be a substitute for schools or society with clear teaching in the home or in the congregations of God?

4. God often sends some episodic shakeups in culture, or in the life of a nation, to get our attention. Can you think of any such times in our history when God has moved to do the same?

5. How is Zerubbabel a "Signet Ring" and a sign of the coming Messiah?

6. How many times can you recall that Israel responded in her history as quickly and firmly as she did under the preaching of Haggai?

Lesson 11

ZECHARIAH

The Prophet of the First and Second Coming of Messiah

The prophet Zechariah is the penultimate book of the twelve Minor Prophets, and it is the longest message of the twelve. It is just a little shorter than the prophecy of Daniel, who is not one of the minor prophets. His writing began in the sixth century, on the eighth month of the second year of King Darius in the year 520 (Zech. 1:1).

Zechariah's work as a prophet overlaps with that of Haggai, for he began his ministry just two months after Haggai gave his first message (Hag. 1:1), and then Haggai gave a second message (Hag. 2:1). Haggai gave two more messages, both on the same day (Hag. 2:18, 20). With the preaching of both these prophets, the nation was finally motivated to begin rebuilding the halted Temple construction again in 520, after it had been stopped for 16 long years.

The Four Main Sections of the Book

In the first eight chapters of Zechariah's prophecy, his message has four divisions: a solemn call for the people of Israel to repent and return back to the Lord (1:1–6); eight visions that all came on the same night (1:7–6:8), ending with the symbolic act of crowning Joshua as priest-king in 6:9–15; a series of four proclamations by the prophet in answer to the questions about the number of times Judah should observe a fast (7:1–8:23); and another series of two important predictions, one focused on the first coming of Messiah (9:1–11:17) and another on Messiah's second coming (12:1–14:21).

Zechariah's message began as already mentioned in an initial message in 1:1–6, which was a solemn call for the nation to repent and turn back to the Lord. This was followed by a section of six chapters (1:7–6:15), which were concluded by Zechariah's receiving a gift of gold and silver from the captives in exile, with instructions for him to design a symbolic crown for Joshua the High Priest (6:9–15). These eight visions in 1:7–6:8 came after Haggai's final messages (Hag. 2:18, 20), all eight of which came to him in a vision in one night (1:7).

Then these six chapters in the front part of Zechariah's book were followed by transitional chapters 7–8, which dealt with questions posed by a delegation sent to Zechariah about the number of times they should hold a fast to the Lord. They posed these questions to Zechariah on the fourth day of the ninth month in the fourth year of King Darius.

The final six chapters in Zechariah appear without a timeline, but they are from a much later time in his ministry. Chapters 9–11, as noted, focused on Messiah's first advent, while 12–14 focused on Messiah's second coming at the end of history.

The Man Zechariah

Zechariah's name means "God remembers." The name no doubt reminded the people of Israel that God had not forgotten them during the 70 years they spent in captivity in Babylon. Like some of his fellow prophets, Zechariah also seems to have come from a Levitical priestly line, for he is described as the son of Berekiah, who was the son of Iddo (1:1). If the Iddo who appears as Zechariah's grandfather is the same individual as the Iddo in Ezra 5:1 and 6:14, then Zechariah may have served in the dual roles of priest and prophet, as did other prophets such as Jeremiah and Ezekiel.

Zechariah is also called a "young man" in 2:4 by an angel. His father Berekiah seems to drop out of the scene quietly and quickly, and may have died early in his life, thus making it necessary that Zechariah fill his place as a priest in the rotating cycle of priests who served in the Temple.

The second part of Zechariah's message centered around two "burden" passages in chapters 9–11 and 12–14. The first "burden," as noted, featured the arrival of Messiah in his first advent (9:1–11:17). The second "burden" message appeared in 12:1–14:21, but it focused on events that would occur in connection with the second coming of Messiah.

Foundational to all these glorious prophecies about the future, Zechariah was given an important message for the nation three months before he received the eight night-visions. In this initial charge, which

God commanded him to give to the nation of Israel, came a strong call to repent and turn back to the Lord (1:1), an invitation to the people of God. This call is one of the strongest and most intense spiritual calls to repentance anywhere in the Old Testament in 1:1–6. Both Haggai and Zechariah summoned God's people to repent and seek him in a revival, for the nation must have an internal cleansing before they took up the task once again of rebuilding the Temple. Israel had to learn the lessons of history (1:4), or she would be sentenced to repeat the identical lessons all over again if they did not repent. Life was so short, for all would die after just a brief period of living (1:5). However, God's word could be depended on, for had that word not been accurate in the past to do what it had threatened or promised to do (1:6)? So, the message to Israel was to turn back to the Lord in full repentance of their sins and in faithful obedience to what he had commanded. This clearly was the will of God, urged Zechariah!

The Message of the Eight Night-Visions

As already noted, Zechariah was given a series of eight visions all in one night. These came three months after the initial message given to him (1:1–6). Each vision had a clear message for the people of Judah, as well as a message for the nations of the earth: either punishment for unbelief or deliverance and salvation for all who believed the Lord were the options for all humankind. Which would it be?

In the first vision, the angel rode on a red horse (1:8) and behind him were red, brown, and white horses. But the riders each disappointingly reported that "all the earth is resting quietly" (1:11). This led to the obvious question: "How long will you [God] withhold mercy from Jerusalem?" (v. 12). God's answer was that he had indeed been angry with Israel and Judah; however, the Gentile nations had taken things too far as they administered more of God's judgment on Israel than he had permitted (v. 15). But the people of Israel should rest assured that God will once more choose Jerusalem and he will intervene on their behalf (v. 17). This first vision will be matched in a companion vision in the eighth dream, so they should be viewed together, but we will view each of the eight visions in order.

In the second night-vision, the prophet was given a picture of four horns (v. 18) that were used to scatter God's people. The "horn" was often used as a metaphor in the Bible for military or administrative power and strength. These horns were followed by four "smiths," who each attacked the "horn" that had preceded them (vv. 20–21), for God would judge each horn from among the hostile Gentle powers by his law and his command (v. 21c).

The third vision, a companion that matches the second one, came to Zechariah on that same night. In this vision, he saw a man with a surveyor's line stretched out over Jerusalem. This vision promised that so glorious would our Lord's return to this earth be that it would affect the city of Jerusalem (2:1–9). That meant Jerusalem would extend far beyond its present boundaries into a new dimension of the future blessings bestowed on that city (vv. 10–13). At the heart of this vision was the divine promise that a "wall of fire" would surround the Jewish nation, thus reversing the tragic and previous departure of the glory of God from the Temple as his divine glory ascended back to heaven, for evil had gotten too far out of hand. For this reason, the glory of God left the Temple and this earth only to return in that future day (Ezek. 43:5).

Together, the fourth and fifth visions form the apex and the central twin visions of the eight night-visions given by God. Joshua, the High Priest in that day, stood before the Angel of the Lord. But Joshua was dressed in "filthy clothes" as he stood there, besmirched with his sins, making his clothes unsightly, defiled, and unholy. Satan, in his traditional role of accuser, stood by Joshua's right hand to accuse him, with a readiness to blast Joshua for his sins, a work Satan was so accustomed to doing, of bringing charges against all believers (3:1). But before Satan had a chance to blast off and accuse Joshua the priest (vv. 3–4), Satan was rebuked outright as God affirmed his continuing support of Jerusalem (v. 2), thus Judah's High Priest was like "a stick snatched from the fire" (v. 2b). The Lord expanded his promise of the restoration of the nation of Israel in the future (vv. 8–10), for God would carry it out all in "one day," i.e., the cleansings of the nation in a national repentance and revival, when the nation looked with deep sorrow and mourning on the One they had previously pierced as they sorrowed for him like one cries over the loss of one's only son (12:10). That day would come on one spectacular day in the future.

The fifth night-vision (4:1–14) in this chiastic arrangement forms the other half of the apex and the twin central message of the eight visions.

The fourth vision had focused, as noted, on the ministry of Joshua, while this vision focused on the governor Zerubbabel. Zechariah teaches three principles: God's work can only be accomplished by his Spirit (4:1–6); God's work must not be despised for its apparent small beginnings (vv. 7–10); and God's work values people more than institutions (vv. 11–14). As Zechariah was shown a lampstand of solid gold with a bowl on top, holding seven lamps with oil for its flames, he was shown that oil came from two olive trees on either side. The message to Zerubbabel was this: "Not by might nor by power, but by my Spirit says the LORD Almighty" (v. 6). He would be energized by the oil of the Holy Spirit.

Vision six (5:1–4) was a twin message with vision seven (5:5–11), just as visions two and three and three and four were twin visions. In the sixth vision, a flying scroll was unfurled, having the precise measurements of 30 feet by 15 feet. These were the identical dimensions of those of the porch on the Tabernacle and the Temple (Exod. 26:15–28; 1 Kings 6:3). Thus, the strong inference was that judgment must begin at the entrance to the house of God.

Two kinds of evil workers are warned in this scroll: thieves and perjurers, representing the whole law of God. Judah was not to tolerate such wickedness in their midst; Israel must turn from all unrighteousness!

The seventh vision depicted sin and iniquity in the shape of a woman, as "wickedness" in Hebrew is in the feminine gender. Sin was now depicted as being encapsulated in an *ephah*, or bushel, and sealed with a lead disc. It was carried aloft by two women to the land of Shinar, the land of ancient Babylon, where it will be kept concealed for a time (Gen. 10:10; 11:2; Dan. 1:2).

The final night-vision is in 6:1–8, corresponding to vision number one. Here four war chariots emerge this time, not from any valleys in Israel (as was the case in vision one), but from two bronze mountains (v. 1). This time there is no report of peace and tranquility, as was the disappointing news in vision one; instead, there were the horrors of martyrdoms resulting from a battle (as symbolized in the red horses' war chariot), some victories (as depicted in the white horses' war chariot), a famine (as seen in the black horses' chariot) and a mixture of death and victory (represented in the dappled horses' chariots). The black and white teams of horses went to the north country, while the dappled team of horses went to the south.

A Delegation of Three Men from Babylon

Three men came from their place of exile carrying a special gift of gold and silver from the exiles in Babylon. The prophet was to fashion an elaborate crown from this gift and place it on the head of Joshua and crown him as priest and king. This was used to introduce five Messianic promises: the promise of a coming Davidic king (v. 12b); the promise that this Davidic person would be called the "Branch" who would "branch out" as he was elevated in significance and as he prospered under the good hand of God (v. 12c); the promise that this Davidic "Branch" would build the "man Branch" who would then take his place as he sat and ruled from his throne (v. 13b); and the promise that this Davidic person would be a priest on his throne (v. 13d; see Ps. 110:4).

The crown mentioned in v. 11 would be stored "for a memorial in the Temple of the LORD" v. (14) as a reminder of the gift sent by the captives and as a testimony to the coming union of priest and king all wrapped up in the one office and the one person of the Messiah.

The men of Bethel had also sent another delegation, manned by Sharezer and Regem-Melech, together with their men to ask Zechariah about the feasts they had been observing in chapters 7–8. Interestingly, God had commanded the people of Israel to observe only one day of fasting, on the day of Yom Kippur, the "Day of Atonement," but the nation had exceeded that command by adding four additional days of fasting to the single day beside the one that God had authorized. Their question was this: Did God want them to continue to mourn and fast on these other four days as well? As the exiles had designated these days of lament and mourning, they were set aside for times such as these: a day to observe the destruction of the Temple in the fifth month (7:3); a day to observe the breaching of the walls of Jerusalem in the fourth month (Jer 39:2); the day when the Governor appointed by the Babylonians, named Gedaliah, was unmercifully murdered in the seventh month (2 Kings 25:25; Jer. 41:1–2); and the day the siege of Jerusalem began in the tenth month (2 Kings 25:1–2; Jer. 39:1).

Zechariah responded to the four questions with four proclamations contained in four questions to be used to search their own hearts:

1. Are you serving yourselves or God by such fasts? (7:1–7)

2. Are you Listening to yourselves or God by this fasting? (7:8–14)

3. Are you believing a lie or the truth in times of fasting? (8:1–17)

4. Are you ready for the future? (8:19–23)

The First Burden – Dispossessing the Gentile Powers of the Land

Both 9:1 and 12:1 contain the headings of "A Burden," which is mostly rendered in our day as "An Oracle." But the Hebrew verb behind this noun is *nasa`*, which means "to lift up" or "to bear," hence the Hebrew noun *massa`* has the better meaning of "a burden." Since these passages consist of "threats or judgments" from God, and as *massa`* is never followed by the genitive of the speaker, it is best to render it as "A Burden." More than an "oracle," these messages began with a word of a coming judgment!

Ordinarily, the territory of Israel was affirmed to extend from "Dan to Beersheba" (Judg. 20:1; 1 Sam. 3:20; 2 Sam. 17:11). However, in addition to the Lord's judgment, he would, in this bright depiction of the land of Israel in a future day, lengthen Israel's borders to include large parts of Syria, Phoenicia and Philistia in that future day.

The first place against which God gave a "burden" was "the land of Hadrach" (9:1), a site not mentioned in Scripture but instead in an Assyrian inscription where it is called "Hatarikka," a city and country north of the city of Hamath on the Orontes River, south of Aleppo. The second city cited in this "burden" message was Damascus (9:1c), capital of modern Syria, followed by the city of Hamath on the Orontes (9:2).

The three chapters of this first "burden" section form a type of triptych in which the two chapters of 9 and 11 describe the Lord acting as a divine warrior against Israel's enemies, while the central panel of chapter 10 deals with the coming Messianic Kingdom. In the Lord's military campaign, he will move from Syria to the coastal towns of Tyre and Sidon, as he subjects them to judgment and fights to protect Jerusalem from its attackers,

Four of the five traditional cities of Philistia (Ashkelon, Gaza, Ekron and Ashdod), after they hear what God has done to Tyre, will be frightened, for the Lord will deal with their pride (9:6b). The victorious march of God will conclude at his house in Jerusalem (9:8). Two expressions in this verse link the first eight chapters of Zechariah with those coming in the last six chapters; 9:8c, "Never shall an oppressor overrun my people" with 7:14, and 9:8c, "for now I am keeping watch with my eyes," with the words in 4:10b.

The arrival of Israel's king is announced in 9:9–10, for not only do they speak of his arrival (9:9a–c) but speak of his character (9:9d–f) and his disarmament of the nations of the world (9:10a–c), plus his own external Kingdom as he speaks peace to the nations (9:10d–f). The people of Jerusalem are urged to join in a spontaneous celebration over the arrival of the Lord, as did Psalm 98. This joy was pointed to in Zechariah 3:14–15 and 2:10. This coming King would be "just," and he would uphold "righteousness" as he brought in salvation with him.

Indeed, he would come in his "humility" riding on a donkey (9:9e–f), the preferred mount of princes in the Ancient Near East (Gen 49:11; Ezek. 21:27). The Gospel writers Matthew (21:2–7) and John (12:12–15) applied these verses from Zechariah 9:9–10 directly to Yeshua's triumphal entry into Jerusalem on the first Palm Sunday. However, Messiah will come a second time, when he will abolish all weapons of war, including the horse and the chariot, as well as the "battle-bow" (9:10a–c).

That coming Kingdom of God will be populated by released captives that demonstrate three things: the power of the blood of the covenant (9:11–13; Exod. 24:8), the success of the armies under the theophany of the Divine Warrior (9:14–15a), and the beauty of the eschatological banquet for the released captives (9:15b–10:1). This victorious day will be made possible by the blood of a substitute that was poured out on the ground to pay the debt owed by those who were forgiven. This will free the prisoners from prison (10:11c). A banquet is then set up for the freed (9:15b–c).

Punishing Corrupt Shepherds and Regathering Israel

God would also deal with the corrupt shepherds (10:2–5), as he provided new leadership, which would be modeled after himself. He who was "the Cornerstone," "the Tent-Peg," and the "Battle-bow" (10:4) would indeed provide the model for every godly ruler in that day (v. 4a).

Just as a shepherd ordinarily signals for his sheep to get ready to move out with a blast from his whistle, so God will whistle for his people, when the time has come for him to regather them in the land of Israel (v. 8). God will bring Jewish people back from all over the world, including Egypt and Assyria (10:10). Then they will walk in the power and name of the Lord.

The Collapse of Lebanon and Bashan, and the Story of the Two Staves

Three metaphors are used for shepherd-leaders: trees, lions and shepherds, symbolizing Lebanon to Israel's north and Bashan to Israel's northeast (11:1–3). Lebanon was renowned for its magnificent cedar trees; Bashan was as famous for its stately oaks. God commissioned Zechariah as a good shepherd, who carried out his duties even though the sheep of Israel were slated for slaughter (v. 4). Zechariah took two shepherd-staffs. He named one "Beauty/Grace" or "Favor" (pointing to peaceful relations Israel would have with foreign nations), and the other he named "Union," pointing to a coming reunion of Israel's northern and southern kingdoms (11:7).

Despite Zechariah's attempts to govern the people of Israel, they just flat out rejected his leadership (11:8b–9). He had to remove three shepherds (11:8–9). As a result of the people rejecting Zechariah's leadership, God would raise up a worthless leader who would not care for his flock, seek the young, heal the injured or feed the healthy (11:16). Who these three worthless shepherds were is impossible to know, but clearly the flock of Israel are being oppressed by their own Jewish leaders, who in collaboration with some Gentile leaders will also assist them in their bad actions in that future day. It is too bad that when God offered to help these people by giving them a good leader, they rejected him and chose instead a most oppressive one.

The Second Burden – A Cleansing of Judah of Foreign Invaders

The events described in chapters 12–14 form the second "burden" message, all said to occur "in that day," a phrase that occurs 17 times in these three chapters and points to the end-time of history on earth! Likewise, "Jerusalem" occurs 22 times, and "nations" appears 13 times.

The verses in this chapter teach that Israel will be delivered from a future attack from the nations by a sudden intervention of the Living God on behalf of his people Israel! God announced himself as the Creator of everything and the One who formed man's spirit (12:1b). The tables are turned against Israel's enemies, as "all nations of the earth are gathered against" Jerusalem for earth's final battle "in that day" (12:3). Jerusalem will not budge but be as "immoveable [as a] rock," and all who try to lift that rock will herniate themselves (v. 3b) as God sends "panic" and "madness" to the attackers of Jerusalem. In fact, it will be clear that "the battle is the LORD's" (1 Sam. 17:47) as never before, for it will be especially and dramatically clear in that end day as Jerusalem will be delivered by the hand of God.

Mourning Over the One the People Have Pierced

On the heels of describing the marvelous victory God will give in that day (12:1–9), Scripture now names two mercies he will dispense: a spirit of grace and supplication (12:10–14), and a new cleansing from sin and all uncleanness (13:1). As God generously pours out his Spirit on the house of David and on the inhabitants of Jerusalem, this spirit of grace and supplication will be part of a most astounding event that will take place. Zechariah 12:10b is usually rendered as follows:

> They will look on Me, the One they have pierced, and mourn for Him as one mourns for an only child and grieve bitterly for him as one grieves for a firstborn son.

But this translation is sharply contested by many Jewish scholars. For example, the Jewish Publication Society rendered this:

> They shall lament to Me about those who are slain, wailing over them as over a favorite son and showing bitter grief, as over a first-born.

The hardest translation issue for many Jewish interpreters is that the words "Me" and "Him" refer to the same person in this passage. To get around this grammatical surprise, these Jewish interpreters declare that it is impossible to pierce God, for he is spirit and not flesh and blood (see Isa. 31:3; John 4:24). But the critical point here is that Yeshua is the Messiah, who became flesh for us (John 1:14), yet he was at the same time One with the Father in essence and being. The words are so indisputably clear that Israel will one day come to its senses and look on Yeshua, whom they allowed to be pierced on the cross in his crucifixion when many had shouted "Crucify him! Crucify him!" In the last day, that same nation will weep bitterly over what they once demanded. In fact, the mourning in that day will be so great, it will be like the mourning that overtook the nation in the plain of Megiddo at Hadad Rimmon (12:11b), when the good and young king Josiah was tragically killed by Pharaoh's troops at only 39 years of age! (2 Kings 23:29; 2 Chron. 35:25) Once again, in some future day, a similar time of national mourning will overtake the nation, but God will open a fountain of cleansing for sin of all, beginning with the house of David, and reaching down to the inhabitants of Jerusalem (13:1).

Cleansing the Land of the False Prophets

On that coming day of the Lord, God would banish the names of idols and the counterfeit prophecies of the false prophets from the false prophets who gave the people the message they wanted to hear (13:2). God would expose these frauds for what they were!

These fakes were so offensive that they will go to all lengths to disguise their former connections with other fraudulent prophets, as shown by the "wounds on [their] hands" (13:6). They will lie by saying that they got these marks *not* from indulging in false actions as false prophets, or in the beatings of their own flesh, but from being in the house of their friends (13:6b).

Striking the Shepherd and Scattering the Sheep

As Isaiah 53:10 taught, "Yet it pleased the LORD to bruise him." so Zechariah 13:7c taught "strike the Shepherd" and the sheep will be scattered. As a result, the sheep are decimated as two-thirds [of those in the land of Israel] shall be cut off and die." The remaining third will come through a time of affliction (13:9a), but they will be refined of all impurities. They shall call upon the name of the Lord and say, "The LORD is my God" (13:9f). The Shepherd here is none other than the Messiah, Yeshua.

Describing the Second Coming of Yeshua

On that great coming day of the Lord, a siege of Jerusalem will take place (14:1a). The Lord will gather all the nations of the world to come against Jerusalem to plunder her (14:2a). The half of the city will be taken into exile, houses will be ransacked, women will be raped, with only one half of Jerusalem left. The horrors of this siege will be monstrous. But then, at last, the Lord will go forth and fight against those nations that have come against his people Israel in the land of Israel (14:3a).

Our Lord will return by touching down on the Mount of Olives, which will immediately split into two, one half moving north and the other south (14:4c–e). This earth-moving event will recall the great earthquake that came in the days of Uzziah king of Judah—an event also mentioned in Amos 1:1. Is this future earthquake associated with the one mentioned in the emptying of the seventh bowl in Revelation 16:18–19?

But just as spectacular will be the ceasing of the lights of the celestial luminaries (14:6) exactly as Isaiah had predicted (13:10; 24:23). It will be a day like no other experienced on Earth. On that day, the Lord will be King over the whole earth (14:9). Water will flow east from the Temple into the Dead Sea and west from that same Temple into the Mediterranean (14:8c; Ezek. 47:1–12; Rev. 22:1). Never again will the peace of Jerusalem be disturbed! (14:11). In fact, the whole landscape all around Jerusalem will be changed because of this seismic activity. So great will this change be that a plain will be uplifted stretching from Geba, six miles north of Jerusalem, with this great uplift of the earth going all the way south to Rimmon, 36 miles southwest of Jerusalem (14:10). That is one huge amount of earth being raised!

Two judgments will be unleashed against the nations that are opposing Jerusalem: a deadly plague (14:15) and a panic among the enemy's troops (14:13). After it is all over, the survivors from the nations of this epic battle engagement will go up to Jerusalem each year to worship the Lord at the time of the Feast of Tabernacles (14:16). Should any nation refuse to go up to Jerusalem, there will be threats of a drought against that nation (14:18). In that day, "Holiness to the LORD" will be inscribed on everything (14:20–21) unclean, and godlessness will be removed from all God's eternal Kingdom.

Conclusions

1. Our Lord summarizes his teaching in this prophet's book by sending a prophet with the name "God remembers," that is, Zechariah. God did indeed remember all he had promised Israel and in that same act of remembering acted as he had promised long ago to do.

2. Zechariah 1:1–6, according to some, is one of the strongest and most intense calls to repentance to be found in the Old Testament.

3. The eight night-visions come to a pinnacle in visions 4–5, with the fourth containing the divine promise that God would remove the iniquity of the land, and the fifth promising with the symbol of the olive oil flowing continuously into the seven-branched lampstand that it is "not by might nor by power, but by my Spirit, says the LORD." This is one of the great promises of the Old Testament!

4. The exiles send to Zechariah a gift of silver and gold, requesting that it be made into a crown and set on the head of Joshua the High Priest and announced, "Here is a man whose name is 'the Branch,'" who will build the Temple and sit on the throne of Israel.

5. There is coming a future day when all Israel will look to the One they had pierced some time ago in history, and they shall mourn as one mourns for a firstborn son that they lost.

Questions for Reflection and Discussion

1. What do you think was the reason for God's placing his solemn call for Israel to repent at the head of Zechariah's prophecy?

2. What was Israel to learn about where her might and strength would come from for the work God would call her to do in the future?

3. Why was the prophet told to make the gold and silver the exiles sent to Israel into both a symbol of a king's crown and a priest's miter?

4. Why will the coming Messiah be seated on a colt?

5. How can we be so sure that "all Israel will be saved" (Rom 11:26) as it is written in Isaiah 59:20, 21 and 27:9?

6. What is the significance of the Mount of Olives splitting in two parts moving away from each other to the north and south in a future day?

Lesson 12

MALACHI

The Prophet of God's Unchanging Love

The prophet Malachi authored the last book of the "Twelve Minor Prophets," and it is the last book of the Old Testament. His name means "my messenger," "my angel," or "messenger of the LORD."

Malachi preached to what seemed a hostile Jewish audience, for he addressed the cynical, the calloused, the dishonest, the doubting, the disillusioned, and those who were downright wicked and skeptical of the prophet's teaching in their lifestyle. Yet despite such antipathy to his message, this prophet focused on the love of God (1:2).

Malachi begins his book with one of many declarations: "A Burden: The word of the LORD to Israel through Malachi" (1:1). This, of course, was how Zechariah 9:1 and 12:1 also began their messages about the future. So, since these three sections of Scripture begin on an identical note by calling their message a "burden," some presume that these three portions of God's Word were written by three anonymous authors as appendices to the whole Minor Prophets collection. But most do not find this a persuasive argument, for the sections in Zechariah form an integral part of the message of that book, and Malachi has its own internal integrity of thought and message.

The Date and Style of Malachi

Most commentators are satisfied to place Malachi in the post-exilic age along with the prophecies of Haggai and Zechariah, both of whom were prominent instigators in the rebuilding of the Temple. More, since Malachi 1:6–14 and 3:10 assumes the Temple of the Lord already exists, then it is plausible that Malachi was written later than the books of Haggai and Zechariah, who began their ministries in 520. Also, a writer named

Ben Sira authored an apocryphal book, "Ecclesiasticus," which is not part of the Old Testament canon. This was written in 180, where he included a quote from Malachi 4:6 in his work, which showed that it existed certainly by that post-exilic date, if not even slightly earlier. There is one more piece of evidence to note: Malachi 1:3–5 has a historical reference to the fact that the destruction of Edom has occurred already. That destruction was not the one carried out by the Babylonian King Nebuchadnezzar in his campaign against Jerusalem in 586; it was more likely the destruction carried out by the Nabatean Arabs who completely drove the Edomites out of their land sometime between 550 and 400 and replaced the Edomites' occupation of the land with their own Idumean state. Thus, the date for Malachi seems to be close to the times of Nehemiah, for these two writers share many of the same concerns and issues, such as marriage to pagan wives (Mal. 2:11–15; Neh. 13:23–27), neglect of paying tithe to the Lord (Mal. 3:8–10; Neh. 13:10–14), disregard for the Sabbath (Mal. 2:8–9; Neh. 13:15–22), corruption of the priesthood (Mal. 1:6–2:9; Neh. 13:7–9), and an outcry against social wrongs (Mal. 3:5; Neh. 5:1–13).

Malachi, then, may have been a forerunner of Nehemiah, one who paved the way for him and his many reforms. Accordingly, we would date Malachi around 433, when Nehemiah returned to Jerusalem a second time.

Most interpreters regard Malachi as a gem in clarity, simplicity, and directness. This brief has a total of 55 verses. Malachi used a prose format, whereas most of the other prophets preferred to use a poetical format. His style was to use questions in the genre of a disputation. Malachi used many figures of speech, and a goodly number of repeated words such as "says the LORD," which appears some twenty times in Malachi.

The prophet has arranged his book into eight sections, each introduced by a divine declaration, which becomes the theme or thesis statement for the disputation that will ensue. This divine declaration is followed by a question for Malachi's audience, which seems to imply they challenged, or seriously doubted, what had just been announced, followed by the Lord's answer through the lips of the prophet. These rebuttals begin with the formula, "Yet / but you say" in 1:2, 6, 7, 13; 2:14, 17; 3:7, 8, 13. Let us look at God's series of declarations.

Declaration: "I Have Loved You"

This divine announcement becomes not just the theme of this first message from the prophet, but the theme of the entire book. This love toward the people of Israel, surprisingly, seemed to be treated as one in which the people were very dubious about such a claim, since they had just spent 70 years in exile. But the Lord's proof followed in 1:2c–4, where the Lord contrasted his alliance with and his love for Jacob, as opposed to the destiny he had set for Edom. To be sure, Jacob and Esau were blood brothers, but God had chosen Jacob and his descendants as the people through whom the world would receive the good news of the Gospel. It was also based on this covenant that God would restore Israel to their land again in the future. Edom had experienced divine judgment just as Obadiah had predicted, but the reason was because of their sin. Edom had tried to rebuild her devastated property in fallen Jerusalem after a humiliating defeat of her capital, but to no avail (1:4–5). However, the basic difference between Israel and Edom was the love God had for Israel. Israel must look beyond her bad provincialism and observe what was going on in history. Israel must also remember that the Lord will be magnified far beyond Israel's geographical borders (1:11, 14), for that would include Edom as well, if they too repented and came to believe in Messiah.

Declaration: "I Am Your Father and Master"

In these second of eight declarations (1:6), God called Malachi to take dead aim at the priests of his day and deliver a stinging indictment for their careless, haphazard, and profane worship of God. What they were doing was not what Scripture taught about how to worship the Living God! True, Malachi later did enlarge the scope of his denunciations beyond the priests and the nation of Israel as he spoke sharply to all who were either cheats or deceivers, Jew or Gentile, and all who attempted to rip off God by offering a sacrifice that was blemished and unfit for such a high and holy God (1:14).

Malachi taught, "A son [by definition generally] honors his father and a servant his master" (1:6a). But if that is true, then where was the honor and the service God deserved? He is God of gods, King of kings and Lord of lords. But the priests have been giving God a lot of sanctimonious lip-service, but their lives and hearts did not bear any of this out. They were too hypocritical, therefore, they showed they despised the name and reputation of God, so why were they demeaning God and his Son?

When the priests objected to such indictments and demanded he prove it was so, Malachi responded, "[They had] offer[ed] defiled food on [God's] altar" (1:7a). But again, the priests denied such deeds outright. Malachi was equal to their denials, for he pointed to the fact that they had offered the blind, lame, and sick animals as offerings to God (v. 8a–b). Polluted mortals cannot offer pure sacrifices to God, for they simultaneously rejected his Lordship, authority, and honor. It was a downright demeaning of God and a defiling of his name and honor to give him what was second-best and with a heart t far removed from him as well! That is precisely what Cain had done, in contrast to his brother Abel. Cain gave his sacrifices without first giving himself, for God looked first at his heart and then at his sacrifice.

During all this rebuke for the sin of the spiritual leaders, the Lord announced—in great tones of authority that showed the greatness of his name—that the opposite was true. It is as if Malachi had had enough, for the moment, of all their negativity and talk about sin; in his view, it was time to talk about the exalted and triumphant state of God and his reputation! In 1:11 he said:

> "My name will be great among the nations, from the rising to the setting of the sun. In every place incense and pure offerings will be brought to my name because my name will be great among the nations," says the LORD Almighty.

God's name, power and authority would not be limited in its effectiveness just to Israel or Jerusalem, but it would be honored all over the whole earth by all peoples who confessed his name. That name was greater than all other names!

However, to return to the issue of the priests, they were so far out of step with the Living God that Malachi told them it would be better if they had the courage to shut up the Temple doors and stop lighting a fire on the altar, which would be all in vain anyway, for they were just putting on a worthless sham (1:10). Moreover, the priests were plain bored in their words, spirit, and deeds. So, what was the use of all their empty acts?

Declaration: "I Will Curse Your Blessings"

Malachi had charged the priests with contempt over the way they handled the sacrifices of the people in a previous section (1:6–14), but to this he now added that they could expect divine consequences to come on them because they had continued to revel in their sin and refused to quit such acts of rebellion against God (2:1–3). Instead of receiving the promised blessings from the Lord, he would now bring a curse over them, and he would spread "offal" (i.e., animal dung or manure) all over their faces (2:3). These priests had defiled the name of the Lord. Accordingly, he would remove them from his presence along with the manure, entrails and hides of the animals (2:3). Men of God must not toy with the awesomeness of the Lord, lest they too be removed from this office by God.

God had given his covenant of life and peace to the sons of Levi (2:5). They had been instructed that they were to teach this knowledge of God and from their mouths should have come biblical instruction (2:7), but the Levites and priests had turned from God's way and instead, by means of their teaching, they had made many to stumble, because the Levites violated the covenant God made with them (2:8). Therefore, these spiritual teachers and leaders were no more to be respected, as they walked in their own ways and showed partiality in what they taught in the law than any other form of low life (2:9).

Declaration: "I Hate Divorce"

Malachi continued his disputation with his audience by setting another proposition for a response: "Have we not one Father? Did not one God create us?" (2:10). If so, and surely it was, then our Lord wanted to know, "Why do we profane the covenant of our fathers by breaking faith with one another?" (2:10b). Believers cannot just disregard what God had taught in his covenant.

The prophet went on to state that Judah had broken faith with the Lord by breaking faith with one another (2:11). They had done this "by marrying the daughters of a foreign god" (2:11e). In marrying these foreign wives, they were joining themselves to the foreign gods of the women who were unbelievers. If that was so, then what fellowship could those who professed faith in Yeshua have in a partnership with evil?

The people of Israel had committed a second offense in 2:13: They had violated God's covenant by divorcing the wives they had married. Because of this transgression, the Lord refused to accept any gifts of sacrifice from these husbands, who in turn divorced their wives. Access to God's altar would now be blocked by the great amount of mist and fog that had been caused by the tears falling from the wives' eyes. This was because their wives had been jilted by their husbands (2:13b). God had been a party to that marriage covenant, as he was to all marriage covenants, and he did not agree with the breaking of that covenant! The Lord acted as One who had witnessed those marriages, where God had also been a covenant partner with the couple (2:14b–c). This is true even to this day where a couple insist on saying their vows before the gathered church in the house of God, then request that God be one who was a covenant partner to this marriage!

Verse 15 has remained an enigma for many, but the key to understanding it is to correctly identify the identity of the "One" mentioned here. It is not Abraham, as some have tried to render it, but the Lord himself. This text, therefore, asks: Why did God make Adam and Eve to be "one flesh," when he had the power to have furnished that marriage with several marriage partners each? The answer was this: It was because such a plurality of partners would not have been conducive to raising children to the glory of God and the tranquility and peace of that home (2:15b).

Verse 16 is one of the strongest protests of divorce anywhere in Scripture. The text goes on to refer to the "covering" of one's [divorced] partner with violence (v. 16c). This "covering" recalls the story of Ruth and Boaz, where spreading of a garment over another person was an idiomatic expression for proposing marriage to a woman. But when the garment that is spread over a partner is suddenly filled with violence, then the idiom speaks of acting unfaithfully and unjustly to one's partner. No wonder this verse concludes with the caution to guard ourselves against such an action and not break faith with the one whom we shared a marriage covenant with and the Lord who also signed on as a marriage partner in this covenant!

Declaration: "I Will Come Near to You for Judgment"

Malachi's audience was quick to deflect all the charges the prophet had brought against them. In fact, they sarcastically announced: "All who do evil are good in the eyes of the LORD!" They added, "He [must be] pleased [with these evildoers]" (2:17), for it appears he has made so many violators among them. Their final punchline was this: "Where is the God of justice [anyway]?" (2:17d).

To such snobbery and backtalk, God gave a straightforward answer: "Behold, I will send my messenger and he will prepare the way before me" (3:1). Our Lord was not misled by all their talk, for such blabbering had plain wearied him. Such attempts to justify the wicked was "an abomination to the LORD" (Prov. 17:15). It surely was a sin to call evil good (Isa. 5:20).

For such carping and tongue-lashing from sinners, God pointed to his messenger whom he would send, who was none other than the man John the Baptist and the prediction he gave in Isaiah 40:3–5. John would come in the spirit and the power of Elijah the prophet (Luke 1:17), even though John denied he actually was Elijah in the flesh (John 1:21), meaning of course that he was not the final and complete fulfillment of this prediction, even though the scribes of Yeshua's day fully expected Elijah would come back on earth before the second advent of the Lord (Mark 9:12; Rev. 11). Elijah had come once in the flesh (Mark 9:12), but God promised to return in that day in the future to restore all things (Matt. 17:11) in connection with the second coming of Yeshua (Acts 3:21). To use the metaphors of the Bible, the Lord would level the roads and straighten the paths as the spiritual work of repentance and faith came to "clear-up" the ground for his arrival (Ps. 80:9; Gen. 24:31). Then those who asked sarcastically, "Where is the God of justice?" would see for themselves things they never even dreamed of as the Lord manifested his power, rule, and reign over everything!

This messenger spoken of in Malachi, however, who prepared the way, was "the Messenger of the Covenant" (3:1). Fact, he was, simultaneously the Owner of the Temple (3:1c); moreover, he was no one less than Yeshua himself. He is called in Hebrew *ha'adon*, with the article. When `adon* appears in Scripture with the article, it always denotes deity (Exod. 23:17, 34:23; Isa. 1:24; 3:1;10:16, 33), for it too was the name borne by Messiah in Psalm 100:1. The Covenant mentioned here is the same covenant originally made with Eve (Gen. 3:15) and later enlarged with Abraham (Gen. 12:2–3; 15:1–6), with David (2 Sam. 7:1–19), and the New Covenant (Jer. 31:31–34). This Lord would come quickly and suddenly—meaning unexpectedly.

Declaration: "I the LORD Do Not Change"

All during these days, the Lord had remained faithful despite the hardness and the resistance of his people Israel. God had not changed in his work or in his promises. Indeed, God had continued to call for Israel to return to him so he could return to them (3:7).

Once again, the people pulled that dumb act of pretending they did not have a ghost of an idea what the Lord had just charged them with, singing out in effect, "Who, us? We should return? Why should we return?" The Lord had plenty of good reasons why Israel should return. To name just one, they had robbed God of his tithes and offerings (3:8), but now the Lord invited them to "test him [in this matter]" (3:10), for if they would, then they would see God had literally poured out his blessings in such abundance on them that they would have no more room to store up all these blessings (3:10d). He would protect their crops from pests and their plants from prematurely casting off their fruits (3:11). More, all the nations would call Israel "blessed," for she would then be a "delightful land" as God had promised (Gen. 12:2–3).

Declaration: "They Will Be Mine"

These rascals continued to argue that "It is futile to serve God" (3:14). They had jointly concluded it was useless, pointless, and downright unrewarding to serve God, for these obviously were lukewarm claimants to the promises of God who were guilty of what would later be some similar practices found in the church at Laodicea in present-day Turkey (Rev. 3:15–17). So if God spit the Laodiceans out of his mouth, and he said he would, guess what would happen to these perpetual gripers?

While these scallywags were making these impudent charges against God and his claims to truth, there was at the same time another group (3:16a) who responded entirely differently: They "feared the LORD," as they "thought [or better "meditated" or "earnestly reflected"] on his name" (v. 16e), for the "name of God" was precisely where they put their values and their strong confidence. No wonder then that their names were put into a "book of remembrance" (v. 16c), which must have been the same as the book of Life (Ps. 69:28; Rev. 20:12, 15). Our Lord regarded these believers as his "jewels" (3:17)!

Declaration: "I Will Send Elijah the Prophet"

A grand day of the Lord was coming in which God would conclude all of history and fulfill the promises he had made to Israel and the nations of the world. God would consign the wicked to an everlasting torment of "flaming fire" (2 Thess. 1:8). But for the righteous person, God would appear as "the sun of righteousness" (4:2) as he would rise with healing in his wings (4:2). Wow! What a promise!

As Malachi ends his prophecy, he reminds his own to "remember the law of my servant Moses" (4:4). He furthermore reminded them that he would send the prophet Elijah before that great and dreadful day of the Lord, for he would turn the hearts of the fathers back to their children and the hearts of the children back to their fathers (4:5–6).

Conclusions

1. The instruments that God chose through whom he would bless the world were the children of Israel. Jewish people have an advantage over Gentiles, for the Word of God was given first through the Jewish people (Rom. 1:16).

2. The ministry of the priesthood tended to defile the things of God rather than urge the people of Israel to walk his path and heed his word.

3. God promised his love to mortals even as they were in the state of resistance and rebellion against him and his word.

4. Our Lord is unchangeable in his character, person attributes. Thus, he remains unchangeable in his nature and attributes while he can and does change whenever we change in our response to him.

5. Our Lord will again send back to earth his prophet Elijah, who will give a final call to all to repent. John the Baptist was in that line of teachers who would be sent by the Lord, but he was not the promised future Elijah himself, who would come in connection with the second advent of the Lord.

Questions for Reflection and Discussion

1. When mortals offer blind, lame, and diseased offerings to God, what does that tell us about their understanding of and appreciation for who God is?

2. If John the Baptist came only, but mightily, in the spirit and the power of Elijah (Luke 1:17), why did he deny he was indeed that Elijah who was to come?

3. Why do some practitioners claim it is futile and vain to serve the Lord? What are they missing?

4. Based on Malachi's message, what is the biblical view of marriage and the marriage covenant? What is said about divorce, and what do you think should be said on this topic as a Believer?

5. Must all tithes and offerings be brought into the local church as God's authentic storehouse for such tithes and offerings, or can some of those tithes go to support other independent works? Should Believers not support parachurch ministries with their gifts because of this teaching?